OTHER TITLES ON ARTS, CRAFTS, FOLKLORE, NATIVE LIFE

Bibliography of Latin American Folklore: Tales, Myths, Festivals, Customs, Arts, Music, Magic. By Ralph Steele Boggs. Blaine Ethridge reprint of: New York--H. W. Wilson Company, 1940, 109 pp., author index.

Life in Brazil; or, A Journal of a Visit to the Land of the Cocoa and the Palm. By Thomas Ewbank. Blaine Ethridge reprint of: New York--Harper & Bros., 1856, 469 pp., over 100 picturesque engravings. Handsomely printed, bound.

The Death Thorn: Magic, Superstitions, and Beliefs of Urban Indians and Negroes in Panama and Peru. By Alma M. Karlin. Blaine Ethridge reprint of: London--Allen & Unwin, 1934, 346 pp., portrait, glossary.

Estancia Life: Agricultural, Economic, and Cultural Aspects of Argentine Farming. By Walter Larden. Blaine Ethridge reprint of: London--T. Fisher Unwin, 1911, 320 pp. + 48 plates of estancia, field, and camp-town scenes.

History of Ancient Mexico: Anthropological, Mythological, and Social. By Bernardino de Sahagun. Translated by Fanny R. Bandelier from the Spanish version of Carlos Maria de Bustamante. Foreword by Clark Wissler. Blaine Ethridge reprint of: Nashville--Fisk University Press, 1932, 315 pp., frontispiece portrait, bio-bibliography.

Arcane Secrets and Occult Lore of Mexico and Mayan Central America: A Treasury of Magic, Astrology, Witchcraft, Demonology, and Symbolism. (Originally, *Magic and Mysteries of Mexico: Arcane Secrets...*) By Lewis Spence. Blaine Ethridge reprint of: London--Rider & Co., 1930, 288 pp. + 16 plates.

Three Dollars a Year; being the Story of San Pablo Cuatro Venados, a Typical Zapotecan Indian Village. By G. Russell Steininger and Paul Van de Velde. Blaine Ethridge reprint of a book published privately in New York, 1935; 121 pp., 16 plates.

Mexican Popular Arts: A Fond Glance at the Craftsmen and Their Handiwork in Ceramics, Textiles, Metals, Glass, Paint, Fibres, and Other Materials. By Frances Toor. Blaine Ethridge reprint of: Mexico City--Frances Toor Studios, 1939, 144 pp., 88 illustrations, including 16 new in this edition.

Artists and Craftsmen in Ancient Central America. By George C. Vaillant. Blaine Ethridge reprint of: New York, American Museum of Natural History, 1935, 102 pp., bibliography; 161 plates and text illustrations.

WRITE FOR ANNOTATED BROCHURE

BLAINE ETHRIDGE--BOOKS
13977 Penrod Street, Detroit, Michigan 48223

ARTISTS AND CRAFTSMEN

in

ANCIENT CENTRAL AMERICA

THE FEATHERED SERPENT

Detail from relief at the temple of Quetzalcoatl, Teotihuacan, Mexico. Teotihuacan is the site of the first real civilization in the Valley of Mexico. After Lehmann, 1933

ARTISTS AND CRAFTSMEN

in

ANCIENT CENTRAL AMERICA

by

GEORGE C. VAILLANT

Associate Curator of Mexican Archaeology

AMERICAN MUSEUM OF NATURAL HISTORY, NEW YORK, 1935
Republished by Blaine Ethridge--Books, Detroit, 1973

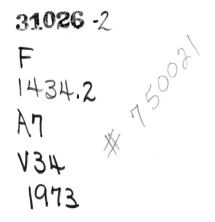
This book was first published as
Number 88 in the Museum's
Guide Leaflet Series

Library of Congress Catalog Card Number 73-78354
International Standard Book Number 0-87917-037-9

PREFACE

The seven articles grouped in this pamphlet are reprinted from *Natural History*. The last six appeared successively as a connected series on the art of pre-Columbian Central America. The first paper, the *Worshippers of the Aztec War Gods*, came out earlier and has been included to give a glimpse of the physical and social background against which these arts flourished.

The purpose of this pamphlet is to provide examples of the extraordinary range of Central American art forms, which are too often buried in technical publications inaccessible to the general public. While there are a number of books which describe vividly and accurately the social customs of the Aztec, Maya, and their neighbors, the high cost of reproduction has prevented a presentation of their art commensurate with its importance. In view of the considerable interest shown in Central American aesthetics, we have tried to give a general picture of art from the artistic rather than the historical point of view.

The American Museum of Natural History has in its halls of anthropology many rare and beautiful examples of human handiwork, chiefly from peoples not blessed by the term "civilized." Since anthropology is concerned with man more as a social organism than as a creator of masterpieces, presentation of exhibits cannot solely be confined to aboriginal fine arts. Yet it is to be hoped that through the media of articles of this nature, the visitor and student will be guided to the riches contained in the halls, the result of centuries of effort by many peoples in many lands to achieve aesthetic satisfaction.

February, 1935.

These articles are reprinted from the following issues of *Natural History.*

Vol. 33, No. 1, pp. 17–30
Vol. 34, No. 2, pp. 117–132
Vol. 34, No. 3, pp. 258–272
Vol. 34, No. 4, pp. 389–402
Vol. 34, No. 5, pp. 485–496
Vol. 34, No. 6, pp. 578–586
Vol. 34, No. 7, pp. 662–673

CONTENTS

BREAST ORNAMENT OF
GOLD WITH TURQUOISE
MOSAIC, MIXTEC CULTURE,
MUSEO NACIONAL MEXICO

The Worshippers of the Aztec War Gods[1]

A Brief Description of Tenochtitlan, the Ancient Mexico City at the Time of the Landing of Cortes

WHEN we realize that the Mayas were in a state of decadence at the time of the Spanish Conquest, and that we recreate much of the splendor of their civilization from the eloquent silence of their ruined architecture, it is well to consider the aspect of the Aztecs who were at their zenith in 1519. Although the Spaniards and their myriad allies so thoroughly razed Tenochtitlan that only a few foundations now remain, there fortunately exists much descriptive information gathered by such eye-witnesses as the Spanish soldiers and the missionary friars, as well as the testimony offered by the documents of the Aztecs themselves.

Bernal Diaz tells how his comrades-in-arms on first beholding Tenochtitlan exclaimed, "It is like the enchantments they tell of in the Legend of Amadis. Are not the things we see a dream?"

This is lyric language from hard-bitten men-at-arms whose chief avocations, while engaged in converting the heathen, lay in acquiring booty and enjoying the charms of dusky Dulcineas. Yet in contrast to the drab towns and tawny hills of Spain, Tenochtitlan must have appeared a Paradise indeed, with its green gardens and white buildings set against the blue of the lakes. "Gazing on such wonderful sights," writes Bernal Diaz, "we did not know what to say or whether what appeared before us was real, for on one side on the land there were great cities and in the lake ever so many more, and the lake itself was crowded with canoes, and in the causeway were many bridges at intervals and in front of us stood the great City of Mexico, and we—we did not even number four hundred soldiers!"

Although socially and governmentally Tenochtitlan was distinctly American Indian, outwardly it appeared the capital

[1] Drawings reproduced from the Codex Florentino, edited by Sahagun in the Sixteenth Century and published by Paso y Troncoso, Madrid, 1907.

MODEL OF THE PYRAMID AT TENAYUCA, FEDERAL DISTRICT, MEXICO

The original temple epitomizes the history of the Valley of Mexico. According to tradition, after the Tenth Century, a tribe of fierce nomads, the Chichimecs, filtered into the Valley and brought about the downfall of its civilized occupants, the Toltecs. The Chichimecs took over elements of the Toltec culture and began a sedentary life. Later, other tribes like the Tepanecs and the Acolhuas entered the Valley and, fusing with the Chichimecs, built up a civilization. Finally came the Aztecs, who, absorbing this Chichimec-Acolhua culture, became strong enough to dominate the Valley tribes.

At Tenayuca six temples were found superimposed, the upper two of typical Aztec architecture. Excavations near by revealed three layers of pottery, the upper of Aztec date, the second probably to be correlated with the Tepanec-Acolhua people, and the crude styles of the lowest layer assignable perhaps to the Chichimec. While it was not possible specifically to correlate the ceramic styles with the individual buildings, yet it is very probable, to judge from the changes in the profiles of the buildings, that they were made by these successive peoples.

The symbolism of the temple involves the worship of the natural forces governing agriculture. Enough stone ornaments were found to reveal the presence of two temples, one honoring the goddess of the Earth and the other the god of War, who was also connected with the Sun. The serpents ornamenting the sides symbolize the earth, and the two connected with the altars flanking the pyramid represent the 52-year calendric cycle which the Aztecs considered much as we do our century.

The excavations were carried out by the Department of Prehistoric Monuments of the Mexican Government during the years 1925-32 as part of their program of reconstruction and research on their antiquities. In making this model, Mr. Shoichi Ichikawa, of the division of anthropology, followed the plans of Mr. Ignacio Marquina, head of the Department of Prehistoric Monuments, under the supervision of Mr. Hay and Doctor Vaillant.

city of an empire. A bird's-eye view would reveal an oval island connected with the mainland by three causeways which were pierced by bridges and which converged at the center of the city. The edges of the island were fringed by the green of the "floating gardens," while toward its center the shiny white of roof-tops predominated, the green being reduced to the little squares of the patio gardens. Thrust above the quadrate masses of the roof-tops loomed the various clan temples, each set on its pyramid. There were few streets or open spaces in the city, which was gridded with canals crossed by drawbridges, but the plazas of the temple of Tlaltelolco and of the religious center of Tenochtitlan stood out from the pyramids and official palaces clustered about them. There must have been a curiously living quality about this grouping, the temples seeming to ride like horsemen among the serrated ranks of the houses.

A visitor would be struck by the rich variety of the sights were he to transverse Tenochtitlan from south to north. Approaching along the causeway, the

SAHAGUN'S MAP OF MEXICO CITY

A.—GREAT TEOCALLI OF HUITZILOPOCHTLI AND TLALOC. B.—PRIEST OFFERING A SACRIFICE. C.—PRIEST QUARTERS. E.—EAGLE WARRIORS' QUARTERS. F.—BALL COURT. G.—SKULL-RACK. H.—TEMPLE OF XIPE. I.—SACRIFICIAL STONE, POSSIBLY STONE OF TIZOC. K.—TEMPLE OF HUITZILOPOCHTLI, THE ORIGIN PLACE OF WORSHIP OF THIS GOD. LATER BUILDING "A" SUPPLANTED IT. L.—5 LIZARD (DATE) AND STATUE OF MACUILXOCHITL, GOD OF FLOWERS. M.—5 HOUSE (DATE) AND STATUE OF MACUIL-XOCHITL, GOD OF FLOWERS. N.—DANCING PLACES, THREE ENTRANCES TO THE TEMPLE EN-CLOSURE ARE SHOWN IN THE SURROUNDING WALL, WHICH WAS ADORNED WITH SERPENT HEADS

traveler of that time passed first between expanses of open water. Then gradually tiny islands of green appeared, the so-called float-ing gardens, made of masses of mud heaped up from the bottom of the lake and spread on reed rafts. White-clad farmers dexter-ously poled their tiny dugouts through the maze on their way to cultivate their garden truck. These irregular islets merged gradually into orderly groups, where the roots had established anchorage in the lake bottom and made more solid ground. Open water remained only in the narrow canals. Save for the broad causeways, roads there were none, and along the waterways one saw in increasing numbers boatloads of produce headed in toward the city. Here and there among the green one caught glimpses of thatched roofs and wattled walls, the huts of the farmers. Then adobe walls of more substantial dwellings began to encroach on the gar-dens, and the waters of the lake shrunk to a canal following the roadway. The adobe walls gradually were replaced by the fronts of houses plastered white or with the rich dull red of powdered pumice. For the first time the visitor realized how the city ex-panded through the artificial creation of beds of vegetation which in solidifying bore first a crop, then a modest hut, and finally became integral with the masonry of the city.

The causeway had now changed from a simple means of communication into the social complexity of a principal street. Since canals took the place of roads, space for a saunter was so rare that the causeways were as much recreation grounds as arteries of traffic. Thus people out to see the sights, people on errands, people on the way to the myriad functions of religious import swallowed up the long lines of trotting carriers who, bowed under their burdens, went to the city with produce and tribute, or left it with goods for barter. Outside the city limits the ant-like streams of laden folk had been but rarely relieved by the rare passage of a civil functionary, all feathers and pomp in his litter, or of a stern merchant with a handful of fighting men followed by a chain of apprentices, show-ing the whites of their eyes as they peered from under the press of the tumplines.

INVESTITURE OF WARRIORS WITH TRAPPINGS OF CASTE

Now could be seen men in rich mantles, sniffing flowers as they watched the milling crowd and black-robed priests whose hair was matted with the blood of self-inflicted penance. There was little sound, there was little hurry, save for the carriers, trotting to reach relief from their burdens. But there was great vitality, that of a multitude of units participating in complex action, knowing each its allotted part but not the substance of the whole.

A glance into the doorway of a dwelling gave relief from the cold-blooded, almost insect-like quality of the life outside. A shaded patio was blocked in with buildings with cool and spacious interiors. Mats and straw cushions on the polished floor welcomed one to repose, while the rhythmic clap of hands and the scrape of stone on stone told that tortillas were being made and corn meal ground in a kitchen at the back. In a corner an elderly man was talking to two small boys, whose serious faces showed that, already conscious of their participation in the tribal life, they heeded their uncle's precepts. In a doorway a fat little girl vainly tried to imitate with her stubby fingers and toy instruments the graceful movements of her mother as she produced fine thread by the cunning manipulation of her spindle. Lolling on a

Photograph from Ewing Galloway

THE "FLOATING GARDENS" OF MEXICO

A scene that might well represent the days before the Conquest. The people in the district of Xochimilco, where this picture was taken, still speak Aztec and live much as did their ancestors

Photograph from Ewing Galloway

THE ZOCALO, MEXICO CITY

The site of the ancient temple enclosure of Mexico as it looks today. The Cathedral is built in front of the great Temple of Huitzilopochtli

cushion, a young man idly smoked, picking thoughtfully at the scarcely healed lobe of his ear, tattered by penitential blood-letting with cactus spine and obsidian blade.

A fiesta was going on in another house and one heard music, the rich vibration of wooden drums and the gay squeal of reed flutes. The patio was full of people gay in the bright colors of their holiday clothes, and the air was heavy with the cloying scent of lilies. The sharp smells of rich sauces cunningly mixed from many peppers embroidered this odor, and occasionally a light breeze wafted the cool, mystic scent of incense. Somebody was celebrating his birthday, since in the background one saw a painted figure adorned with maguey paper representing the titulary deity for the day. A little apart from the feasters, who partook of their entertainment with dignified pleasure, clustered a group of old men whose clownish gestures and burlesque solemnity could be easily associated with

the cups that a slave was industriously filling for them. Not for nothing had they passed through the rigid self-denial of young manhood to be permitted alcoholic indulgence in their old age, whenever a feast came around. A last backward glance revealed the musicians, garlanded with flowers, blowing their flutes and conch shells, while one beat on the head of a cylindrical drum and another the wooden tongues in the side of the two-toned *teponaztle*.

Farther up the street the priests seemed to increase in numbers and more individuals wore the trappings of high office, such as the nodding panaches of quetzal plumes and cloaks the designs of which were worked in feathers like the clan insignia on their circular shields.

Presently the causeway ended in a great open square where rose the majestic planes of the pyramids. In the hard, bright light of early afternoon, heat waves joined with smoke of incense in rendering

HOUSE OF WATTLE AND DAUB, USED BY THE
POORER FARMERS

it through the rings set transversely to the walls along the length of the courts.

A circular stone set a short distance away was the scene of a most cruel game. Here on certain ceremonial days a tethered captive was allowed to defend himself with a wooden club against the onslaught of an adversary whose weapon was set with razor-sharp obsidian blades. Sometimes a victim would resist so successfully that he gained a pardon. The great disc of the calendar stone was

indistinct and unearthly the outlines of the temples, and the short, black shadows suggested unspeakable things. Was it imagination or reality, that sickening odor of a filthy butcher shop, in bitter contrast to the immaculate pavement of the courtyard? Imagination was too personal a sensation for an Indian community and the great block of the skull-rack gave the answer. Thousands of skulls were piled up in orderly symmetry, and the blacks of the eye sockets and nostrils of these sacrificed victims suggested heaps of infernal dice. A few young men were practising in a ball court near by, thrusting at the ball with agile hips while striving to propel

A NOBLE'S HOUSE. NOTE FRESCO AND STONE
COLUMNS

placed vertically on another platform. Carved with consummate mastery of design, it represented the symbolic history of the world. A third great disc, carved on its face and edges, commemorated the far-flung conquests of the War Chief Tizoc.

A sacrifice was to be made. Before a small temple dedicated to one of the gods, a group was gathered, some in the gay panoply of merchants and others wearing the sinister black of the priesthood. Among them, tightly-pinioned, stood a slave, who looked unseeingly about him, resignation, not fear, in his face. The priests rushed him up the steep steps to the temple, the merchants following at

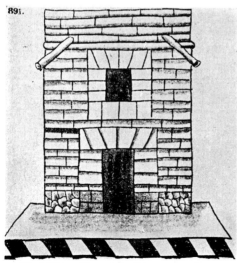

TWO-STORY HOUSE OF STONE AND ADOBE

more leisurely pace. Two priests, seizing the slave by either arm, forced him backward while two others pulled his legs out from under, until his body curved, belly upward, over the altar. A fifth priest dragged his knife in a long sweep from the breast-bone to the base of the stomach and, reaching into the aperture, with a dexterous twist tore out the heart. They burned this on the altar, and the mer-

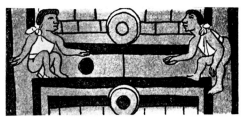
A BALL COURT. THE POINT OF THE GAME IS TO PASS THE BALL THROUGH THE RINGS

18.
BOYS GOING TO SCHOOL. NOTE THAT THE PARENTS WEAR THE DRESS OF POOR FOLK

chants, swinging long ladles of smoking incense, chanted their thanks for a safe and profitable excursion to the hot country.

Paying no attention to this pious little scene, knots of chiefs were converging on a large building at a corner of the plaza. The War Chief Montezuma was planning an attack on a neighboring town remiss in its tribute and there must be a gathering of the clan leaders. Adorned with helmets like the heads of jaguars, eagles, and wolves, girt with armor of wadded cotton brocaded in many colors or embroidered with feathers, their faces set with nose and lip ornaments of jade and gold, these fierce-faced chiefs passed through the door, but before entering the council chamber they stripped off this finery.

Then bare-headed and barefooted, with downcast eyes, they made their way before the throne where sat the slim figure of Montezuma the War Chief, who was simply dressed but for the jade earrings and gold crown of his exalted office.

The austerity of the council chamber was not borne out by Montezuma's other apartments, which contained all the appurtenances of luxurious potency. Magnificent quarters were occupied by the War Chief's two wives and his many concubines. Kitchens and store houses were spread over another great space, for

79.
WARRIORS. NOTE RICH TRAPPINGS AND VICIOUS CLUBS OF WOOD, TOOTHED WITH OBSIDIAN

A PRODUCE MARKET. THE NEAT ARRANGEMENT OF WARES MAY BE SEEN IN ANY MEXICAN MARKET TODAY

not only were some three hundred guests served at each meal but also a thousand attendants and guards. In contrast to the profusion within, outside the kitchen door squatted patiently a meager group of countrymen from whose carrying bags swayed the mottled heads of trussed turkeys to be offered to the larder.

Other apartments in Montezuma's palace contained the tribal treasure composed of the tribute wrung from many pueblos. Gold, jade, rich feather mantles, baskets of produce were heaped in abundance. Clerks were listing the goods to see that each subject town had contributed its

quota, or calculating the share that should be turned over to the various clan stewards. Another patio presented a more animated scene. Here acrobats were practising their feats and poor, warped dwarfs were composing grosser contortions to win a chiefly smile. In another set of buildings was housed the zoo, where serpents undulated sluggishly, and where from behind wooden bars peered the greedy, yellow eyes of jaguars and ocelots. In a side room, a human

PUNISHING MALEFACTORS. FOUR JUDGES SUPERVISE EXECUTIONS BY NOOSE AND CLUB

hand projecting from a basket of raw meat showed how the bodies of some of the sacrificed victims were utilized.

Extending north from this great plaza, which even today is the center of the city, stretched the highway to Tlaltelolco. This wide road with a canal beside it was filled with the same indecisive multitude that filled the southern artery. The sinking sun had brought people out on their roof tops. Some leaned over parapets to watch the throng below, even as idlers squatting in a shaded bit of the street took equal interest in the slow movements of the householders above them.

A path and canal debouching into the main avenue led to a small square, in the

A GROUP OF JUGGLERS. OBSERVE THE HUNCHBACKS IN THE LOWER ROW

STAIRWAY OF THE PYRAMID OF TENAYUCA
Near Mexico City. This is an excellent illustration of the dramatic quality of Aztec architecture

center of which loomed a pyramid. From the patio of a large building shrill cries arose and the dull clash of wooden instruments. Within, a number of boys were receiving instruction in the manual of arms. Each equipped with a small buckler and a flat club of wood, they learned the art of cut and parry under the scornful eye of a warrior. They dealt and received severe blows, but the clubs were not toothed with the wedges of obsidian, the volcanic glass that made hand-to-hand combat so vicious in war. Another group were practising with the atlatl or throwing stick. The marksman laid his spear along a narrow wooden trough hooked at the farther end, the nearer end being grasped in the hand. By lengthening the arm in this way it was possible to attain a greater propulsive force.

A less animated scene took place among the boys of the religious training school on the other side of the plaza. Their little legs and faces lacerated by maguey spines, their bodies thin from penance, and their eyes dulled by the monotony of self-denial, these children were chanting strophes from a ritual. The preceptor who led the singing showed in his own scarred and emaciated body that the propitiation of the gods was a relentless and never-ending task. Priest, chief, warrior, or husbandman, every Aztec from boyhood on, spent much of his life either in a kind of beseeching penance to ensure his future or in a state of grateful atonement for not having had a worse past. The Aztecs lived on intimate if uncomfortable terms with the supernatural powers.

Another aspect of this lack of individualism was to be seen in the tecpan or clan building. Here elders of the clan were arranging the affairs of the group. One old man by means of maps adjusted a question of land tenure between two contesting families, making his judgment on the basis of how much land each family could cultivate by its own efforts.

TRADE FROM THE HOT COUNTRY. JAGUAR SKINS, JADE, AND FEATHERS ARE OFFERED FOR SALE

Another old man was distributing some pottery, given up as tribute from a town across the lake, to some of the poorer members of the community. None of these people bestowed more than an occasional glance into the back courtyard where an adulterer was being stoned to death by the members of the affronted family. Urban existence contained too many interests and life was too cheap for them to view as an excitement the inevitable result of wrongdoing.

In many such centers each phratry regulated its own affairs. The great plaza where Montezuma had his palace and where the gods were worshipped in many temples was for the use of all the clans together. Yet in spite of the importance of this center, the great plaza of Tlaltelolco near the northern edge of the island was almost as striking. The self-contained nature of a Mexican tribe did not diminish the governmental functions of a conquered people, who were supposed to furnish fighting men and tribute, once they acknowledged the sway of a superior power. Thus the recently conquered Tlaltelolco had a communal center as

TRADE FROM THE HIGHLANDS. GOLD, COPPER, OBSIDIAN, AND MANTLES ARE OFFERED IN EXCHANGE FOR TROPICAL PRODUCTS

majestic as that of Tenochtitlan. It seemed more dramatic to Spanish eyes, perhaps because its great temple to Huitzilopochtli was thrust into prominence by the wide spread of the market place, while in Tenochtitlan the great buildings were so close together that it was hard to gain an impression of their size.

The open space was divided into two sections. A large area of smoothly polished pavement was bordered by arcades which sheltered many of the merchants. At one edge was a basin opening from the canal beside the northern causeway, where the boats bringing goods and produce could find an anchorage. Each kind of product was concentrated in a special place. Thus one section was devoted to vegetables, and compactly squatting women sat watching their goods, which were arranged in symmetrical heaps on woven mats. In

A SLAVE FAMILY. THE BARS ACROSS THE NECKS ARE THE SIGN OF BONDAGE

another section cotton mantles were being sold, some being spread to show the full design, and others neatly folded. Elsewhere was a row where tools were for sale, obsidian blades, spindle whorls of pottery carved and burnished, spoons of deer horn, bodkins of bone, and a few copper axes. A brilliant mass of color characterized the row of the feather salesmen. Some sold merely bunches of the feathers, the green of the trogon and the multicolored plumage of the parrots, while at the booths of the others cloaks, mats, and shields gave evidence of charming fancy and patient toil. Jewelers displayed ornaments of jade and gold worked into precious rings of filigree or massive, beaten gorgets. It was the jade, however, that caught the envious eye and was produced with furtive circumspection as material of great price. Other merchants sold ornaments of shell, and the pinks, whites, and subtle mottled browns of sea shells contrasted with the rich, dark sheen of the tortoise carapace. At one booth a rich warrior earnestly chaffered with the proprietor for an exquisite pair of earplugs,

GOLD WORKER MAKING A MOSAIC DESIGN LIKE THE BREAST ORNAMENT ON PAGE 5

cunningly inlaid with a mosaic of turquoise and shell.

The smiling whispers and admiring glances of the crowd when at the jewelers' abruptly changed in the slave quarter to appraising stares. Some of the chattels wore wooden collars and stared blankly with brutish eyes. These had reached their servitude through penalties for crime or by capture in war. Others were thin and emaciated, and did not wear the collar of bondage. They had met with misfortune and were selling themselves to ensure food and shelter.

A low hum rose from the market place; there was none of the strident shouting of a European fair. The bargaining for goods was carried on slowly, quietly, but none the less keenly. The Aztecs had no money, so that barter was the usual means of purchase. The cocoa bean, however, had a standard value and this, in equalizing exchanges, performed the nearest approach to the function of currency. Passing through the crowd were warriors who acted as police, and should a dispute arise, they haled the disputants to a court where one of the tribal elders settled the question.

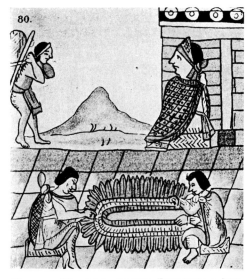

FEATHER WORKERS. IN THE DISTANCE A MERCHANT BRINGS THE RAW MATERIALS FROM THE TROPICS

FARMER PLANTING CORN. NOTE THE USE OF THE PLANTING STICK

Beyond the market was a double line of walls which divided off the religious part of the plaza of Tlaltelolco from the market. Rectangular buildings, with patios in their centers, housed the priests and the various schools and councils of the central organizations of the Tlaltelolcans. Farther on were grouped the main temples of the various divinities. In the center the great temple shouldered its bulk into the sky. There was a skull-rack like the one in Tenochtitlan, and another heap was made of the bones of the victims. Near the great pyramid stood a circular temple, the door of which was built to resemble the mouth of a serpent: the place of worship for the god Quetzalcoatl. The sacrificial block in front was black with the smoke of incense and the encrusted blood of victims. A pile of stone knives and axes gave a sinister indication of what rites were practised there.

Pools of water fed by pipes from the aqueduct gave an impression of quiet peace and the reflections of the temples, distorted by an occasional breeze, intensi-

fied the brooding mysticism of the sacred enclosure. As a relief to the austerity of the scene young girls with downcast eyes slipped back and forth on the various errands of their training school within the enclosure. The great pyramid, that of Huitzilopochtli, the war god, completely dominated the place. Terraces breaking at intervals the line of the sloping sides increased the impression of its size. A wide staircase of one hundred and fourteen narrow steps led up the western side, and so steep was this stair that not until one's head rose clear of the platform, did the temple itself come into view.

The temple was, in reality, two shrines, built side by side, each having stone walls and soaring roofs of wood. Through the right-hand door, one could dimly see the squat figure of Huitzilopochtli carved in stone and then covered with a paste in which were set jade, turquoise, gold, and seed pearls. A girdle of snakes in gold picked out by precious stones adorned its waist, and around its neck hung a string of gold masks with turquoise mosaic. By its side stood the statue of an attendant deity with a short lance and a gold

FARMER STORING CORN FOR WINTER. POTTERY JARS LIKE THOSE SHOWN HERE ARE USED FOR STORAGE TODAY

A Fiesta. Here A Drummer and Singers With Rattles, Flowers, and Feather Fans Make Merry

Musicians Singing a Duet. The Scrolls Here Show the Lilt of Song. Note Details of Drum and Rattle

shield richly decorated with a turquoise mosaic.

In the other temple was an image of Tezcatlipoca, one of the most prominent Aztec gods. Its eyes were inlaid with mirrors of obsidian that gleamed reddishly in the afternoon light. This statue, too, was adorned with gold and precious stones. High in the wooden roof of the temple was a small statue of the god of seedtime. Braziers of incense discharged greasy coils of smoke which plunged into deeper gloom the temples whose walls were already black with the blood of many victims. In dim corners stood heaps of parapherna-

lia, conch-shell trumpets, knives, banners, and baskets of shapeless human hearts that had not yet been placed upon the braziers. The priests gliding in this murk seemed fitting satellites to the diabolic gods they served. In front of the

Priests, Men, and Women Witnessing Human Sacrifices at the Shrine of the Warrior God Huitzilopochtli

temple stood the great drum that was soon to throb across the lake the death throes of a nation.

It was from this point that Montezuma showed Cortes his empire, and Bernal Diaz, who witnessed the scene, has left an unforgettable description, which is the best conclusion to this brief sketch of Tenochtitlan, the ancient Mexico City.

"Then Montezuma took Cortes by the hand and told him to look at his great city and all the other cities that were standing in the water and the many other towns and the land round the lake. . . . So we stood looking about us for that huge and cursed temple stood so high that from it one could see over everything very well and we saw the three causeways which led into Mexico . . . , and we saw the (aqueduct of) fresh water that comes from Chapultepec which supplies the city and we saw the bridges on the three causeways which were built at certain distances apart . . . and we beheld on the lake a great multitude of canoes, some coming with supplies of food, others returning loaded with cargoes of merchandise, and we saw that from every house of that great city and of all the other cities that were built in the water it was impossible to pass from house to house except by drawbridges which were made of wood, or in canoes; and we saw in those cities Cues (temples) and oratories like towers and fortresses and all gleaming white, and it was a wonderful thing to behold!"

CAST OF THE NATIONAL STONE

An Aztec sculpture which might be called a model, since it probably represents the Calendar Stone set on a pyramid. The original is about a meter square and is richly adorned with carvings pertaining to worship of the Sun God.

Temple, Nahua Style, Santiago Huatusco, Vera Cruz. After Dupaix, 1834

The Architecture of
Pre-Columbian Central America

THE art of Central America is as baffling as it is impressive. Completely a product of the Indians of the New World, it cannot be fitted into the customary canons of European aesthetics. The higher expressions of Central American art are far from primitive, the modern American, missing the emotional appeal of his own art, feels something remote and undeveloped in Pre-Columbian civilizations. Yet, since we ourselves are immigrants in a new land who built up our own civilization, the cultural and artistic achievements of previous immigrants, of different race, to the same continent should be as worthy of our knowledge as the culture of the ancient Egyptians, which is part of all our courses in ancient history.

In the preceding chapter we have tried to describe the life in a typical Central American community and in the following pages the art that flourished amid such surroundings, in an effort to bring into sharper focus the more tangible aspects of Central American art. But before we begin to discuss these various manifestations, let us roughly sketch the historical background of these civilizations.

The first immigrants from Asia entered America by way of Alaska toward the close of the last glaciation, and this infiltration of peoples probably continued up to the time of European colonization. Since no traces of Asiatic civilization are found in North America, the cultural plane of which is relatively low, there are no good grounds for assuming that these immigrants brought an art with them. At some time during this population of the New World, groups of people in Central America and northern South America began to develop an agriculture based on

agriculture than the Asiatics, the Central Americans worshipped those natural forces which controlled the harvest, and evolved a religion in their honor.

Photograph by La Rochester, Mexico
PYRAMID OF CUICUILCO, VALLEY OF MEXICO
This oval structure of adobe studded with uncut stone is completely surrounded by the lava flow at the left. It is probably the oldest building in Central Mexico

The broken mountainous country stretching from the Rio Grande to Panama has several distinct climates, according to the altitude. Great forests and mountains tended to isolate inhabited communities. Consequently small groups of people could retain their language and develop dialects as well as evolve distinctive customs and art forms. Some of these tribes developed most sophisticated civilizations, while others lagged, retaining a primitive culture. To thread our way through the tortuous mazes of the cultures of these tribelets is beyond our purpose, nor have we the knowledge to do so even if we wished.

native plants like corn, potatoes, and manioc, which were unknown to the Old World until after the discovery of the New. This food supply is one of the most important proofs that the New World civilizations were uninfluenced by those of the Old. A contact with the Old World close enough to permit absorption of its art styles would also utilize its food plants and domestic animals.

Once a stable food supply was assured them, the tribes in Central America had an opportunity to develop their culture. Perhaps more conscious of the novelty of

Two major artistic developments can be discerned, however, the art of the Maya-speaking people of the low, hot country of Guatemala and Yucatan, and that of the Nahua tribes of the Mexican Highlands. Combinations and transitions between Maya and Nahua art may be seen in the civilizations of the tribes in adjoining regions. Maya art is the aesthetic of a gentle people, whereas Nahua art is the product of a more austere and warlike folk.

The period of Central American art covers the first fifteen hundred years of the Christian era. Previous to that time

Photograph by S. G. Morley
TEMPLE Evii SUB, UAXACTUN, GUATEMALA
This oldest Maya building yet found is made of rubble with a plaster covering. It is a platform without any trace of a temple. Note the masks carved at the sides (See p. 57)

the tribes of Central America were making the slow climb from a hunting stage and inventing agriculture anew, while some of the Old World nations had already embarked on the preliminary stages of civilization. The Maya seem to have been first to produce a really fine art in Central America, but, by the Tenth Century, the Nahua had also developed a concrete aesthetic expression. While in the first ten centuries of the Christian era the Maya were artistically predominant, they afterward began to decline, so that at the time of the Spanish Conquest in 1519, Nahua tribes, like the Aztec and Mixtec, produced the major examples of Central American art.

Having roughly oriented ourselves in time and space, we can now examine the various expressions of Central American aesthetics. We can appreciate a little more clearly the circumstances under which groups of people, without steel tools and without draught animals, were able to create a civilization that glorified not themselves but the gods who permitted them to exist. Living in subservience to their divinities, the Central Americans seemed little interested in their own emotional weaknesses or sentimentality, and this impersonality, often austere, defines their art.

◆ ◆ ◆ ◆ ◆

Architecture, more than any other art, symbolizes the pitiless quality of Central American civilization. However, as coldness also characterizes our own modern buildings, the architecture of the ancient Mexicans and Mayas gives us the most comprehensive approach to their art. We can also understand, since the major architecture of Central America is dominantly religious, how ritualistic and ceremonial requirements permeate the other arts like sculpture, painting, textiles, jewelry, and pottery.

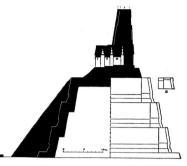

TEMPLE II, TIKAL GUATEMALA,
MODEL AND SECTION

The decorative emphasis has passed
from the platform (p. 21) to the temple
proper. The rooms are mere slits in the
solid masonry mass supporting the roof
comb on which decoration is concentrated. It can be readily seen that the
basic idea is to construct a monument
rather than a place to house a congregation. Temple II is one of the oldest
Maya religious structures, and illustrates one of the fundamental principles
of the religious architecture. The succeeding photographs trace the evolution
of religious monuments like this into
temples. Section after Maler, 1911
(See also p. 56)

Religion was the most vigorous social force in Central America. Priests, not chiefs, governed the various tribal groups, and these hierarchs were ever conscious that they must placate the gods who controlled all natural phenomena. This philosophy caused the tribal leaders to organize ceremonies and establish places of worship in order to cultivate the favor of their divinities. Religious demands so completely absorbed the surplus energy of the Central American people, once they had met their needs for subsistence, that, except in the highest civilizations, one can discern few traces of specific civil government.

Under such conditions it is not surprising that the ceremonial architecture was tremendously developed, while dwelling houses, made of adobe or wattle and daub, were of the simplest nature. Only the Aztecs and their neighbors in the Valley of Mexico seem to have produced a domestic architecture at all complex. Discussion of the artistic evolution of architecture naturally centers around the buildings used directly and indirectly for religious purposes.

We do not know the point of origin for Central American architecture, or whether it had been evolved at a single place or in several. But the most common type of ruin comprises a group of mounds, set sometimes around a central plaza, sometimes without an obviously formal plan. Quite commonly in the mountainous regions collections of mounds are strung along ridges or mesas, which have been graded to provide level surfaces for living and to give a solid basis for the erection of platforms. Very often these terraces and substructures were faced with stone over a hearting of adobe or rubble, when a suitable quarry was readily accessible.

The groundplans of Central American cities differ, but in two respects only — formal or informal grouping. Yet, the arrangement of the plan seems to depend on local conditions of terrain or order of construction, rather than on the scale of cultural evolution. The architecturally very developed Chichen Itza has a haphazard distribution, while the older and structurally much simpler Teotihuacan is most elegant in its orderly design.

Preservation is an extremely important factor in our estimates of architectural values. The stone-faced temple of Yucatan which has resisted the elements seems to us more worthy of admiration than the battered adobe or rubble buildings on the Mexican Highlands which have capitulated to the elements. For all we know there may have been superb buildings of wood representing an interesting and imposing architectural order which, being incapable of preservation, is lost to us. We cannot, then, judge buildings en masse, but must trace by individual temples the course of Central American architecture.

The fundamental idea in Central American architecture was to create a focal point for ceremonies which took place outside the buildings. The temples were seldom intended to *house* congregations, as were the cathedrals of Europe or the great temples of Egypt, nor in shape or purpose do they resemble those colossal mortuary chambers, the Pyramids. Maya and Mexican ceremonial structures were true monuments to the glory of the gods.

In view of this dominant interest, the constant enlargement of buildings is not surprising. Moreover, in several regions, the termination of a fifty-two year cycle was the occasion for renovating all possessions, ceremonial and personal, even

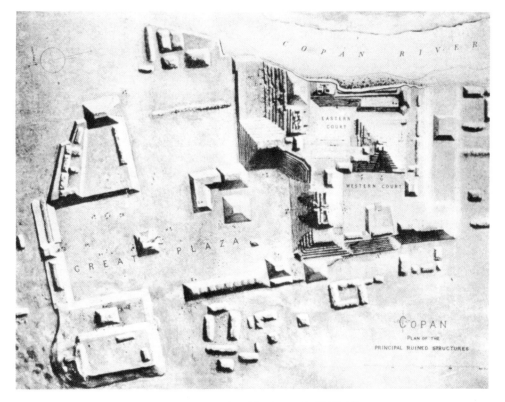

RELIEF MAP OF COPAN, HONDURAS

Showing the plan of this ancient Maya city. Note the amount of grading done before construction of buildings began. After Maudslay, 1899

THE GATEWAY AT LABNAH, YUCATAN

A magnificent example of northern Maya architecture. The corbel vault is composed of overlapping stones which are supported by the weight of the masonry above, and are not united by a keystone, as in the true arch. Photograph by the Department of Historical Monuments, Mexico

to the destruction of household articles used up to that time. This aggrandizement was accomplished in two ways. The simpler method was to build over the original structure, filling in the temple and adding to the platform until both were converted into a foundation on which a new temple could be erected. Due to this custom many buildings that would otherwise have been lost are now preserved within the sheathing of the later additions. The second way was to add a wing or an ell to the original structure, a method of addition well known to us today. Sometimes the two methods were combined.

The two oldest buildings known to us in Central America were platforms, probably without temples. One of these is the oval mound of Cuicuilco in the south of the Valley of Mexico. This was built of adobe bricks arranged in several ascending terraces, and two staircases were disposed at either end. The outside of the structure was faced with river boulders, over which a later enlargement had been made, utilizing lava blocks as a veneer. An altar in horse-shoe shape surmounted the earlier building, but no trace remains of whatever construction crowned the later mound. While it is possible that this earlier altar was enclosed, its size and shape suggest that it was built in the open. The antiquity of Cuicuilco is incontestable, first because a lava flow surrounded the building after it had been abandoned, and second, because the associated objects tie in with the remains of one of the Early Cultures of the Valley.

The other temple, Evii-sub, at Uaxactun in the heart of the Maya country, was a quadrangular structure of rubble coated with a thick layer of plaster. Stairs ascended the sides, flanked by broad buttresses carved into grotesque masks. There was no trace of any construction on top of the platform. The

CHICHEN ITZA, YUCA-
TAN

In this panorama of a late
Maya city may be seen how
formal groundplan was seldom a primary consideration
with the Maya. The temples
of the Mexican period in the
background show a more orderly arrangement than do
the Maya buildings in the fore-
ground. After Holmes, 1895

preservation of this perishable structure
was accomplished by a later platform
which effectively sealed it from destructive natural agencies, such as roots and
rains. That temple Evii-sub is of substantial antiquity there can be little
doubt, as the outer building was associated with some of the earliest time-
markers found in the Maya area.

Both of these early structures were platforms, not temples. The underlying idea
was definitely to attain elevation, and
thus to dramatize the ceremony. The open
summits show that there was no idea of
enclosing the ritual, so that temple construction must have been a secondary
factor. Already we can discern in the
carved surfaces of the Uaxactun temple
the Maya preoccupation with design, and
in the unadorned surfaces of Cuicuilco

the Mexican emphasis on mass and treatment of planes.

The need of a place to house the image
of a god must soon have made itself felt,
and soon the custom of a temple or shrine
surmounting the mound must have arisen.
The earliest Maya temples preserved were
of rubble faced with plaster, and were intended to be seen rather than used. The
carving which had embellished the side
walls of the platform, as at Uaxactun,
was transferred to the temple, leaving the
substructure bare. To receive this decoration a masonry block was built on the roof,
but the weight of this mass necessitated
extremely thick walls to support it. Furthermore, the Maya used a corbel or false
arch, incapable of bearing a heavy weight.
As a result we find massive buildings with
rooms only two or three feet wide.

In time the Maya
learned how to lighten
the burden of the roof-
comb by rearing a narrow
perforated wall directly
above the partition walls
of the temple. By so do-
ing, no weight fell directly on the arch of the roof,
and it became possible to

TEMPLE AT RIO BEC,
QUINTANA ROO

This Maya temple shows the
transition from a religious
monument to a shrine with
usable rooms. The towers are
conventionalized reproductions of the Tikal type of
temple (p. 22), while the
building proper is not unlike
the Yucatan structures shown
above and on page 26

THE "NUNNERY." CHICHEN ITZA

A building of Yucatan Maya type (see also p. 25, upper). Stone is used as facing and elaborate ornament relieves the outer surfaces. Note how this solid construction resists decay and renders possible an accurate appraisal of the architecture. After Totten, 1926

CROSS-SECTION OF THE "NUNNERY"

Showing structural detail and method of accretion. The platform, c, was built to add a second story, d, to the wing at the left of the photograph above. The third story, g, reached by the stair, f, was added later, after filling in one rank of the d series of rooms. After Holmes, 1895

THE CASTILLO, CHICHEN ITZA, A MEXICAN PERIOD TEMPLE

Showing this foreign influence in the dramatic treatment of the stair and the serpent columns and balustrade. The Temple of the Warriors, a notable companion building, is shown on p. 34. Photograph by Department of Historic Monuments

HOUSE OF THE DWARF, UXMAL

Compare the ornate treatment of the ornament on this Maya temple with the simplicity of the Mexican-influenced Castillo above. Note how the portal represents a serpent mouth. Totten, 1926. after Catherwood, 1841

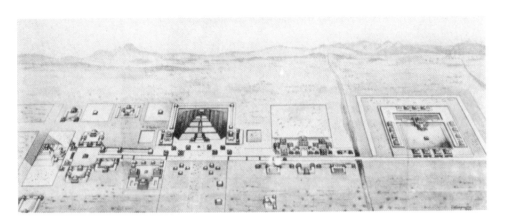

RECONSTRUCTION OF TEOTIHUACAN

In the Toltec city of the Mexican Highlands, groundplan is very important. The temples are grouped in precincts, which in turn are arranged in axes. After Gamio, 1922

PYRAMID OF THE SUN, TEOTIHUACAN

This central structure in the panorama above is made of adobe with a stone facing and was the foundation for a temple. Note the size in contrast with the buildings near by. Photograph by Fairchild Aerial Surveys de Mexico. S. A.

have wider rooms. Once room plan became a primary consideration, it was possible to give the rooms a more varied use instead of confining them to the support of a heavy roof-comb. At Palenque we find an outer and an inner shrine, the latter containing a small sanctuary, and at the Castillo in Chichen Itza an outer corridor surrounds the shrine. The culmination of the temple idea is the great Temple of the Warriors at Chichen Itza and its various annexes. Here the roof-comb was dispensed with, and rows of elaborately carved columns supported a series of arches. This building, strongly affected by influence from Mexico, is the most important Central American example of a temple which afforded space for a congregation within its confines.

TEMPLE OF THE SUN, PALENQUE
The most evolved type of Maya building. Compare the wide rooms here with the narrow slots at Tikal (p. 22). Notice also the shrine in the back room, and the division of the door into a colonnade

The essence of Maya architecture may be seen in the evolution of the offering platform into a pyramid surmounted by an ornamented shrine which finally, through increased knowledge of construction, is developed into a temple. Paralleling this development is that of the associated buildings which presumably were to house the temple staff. Without the necessity of supporting an elaborate ornamental crest, the rooms could be as wide as a corbel vault could conveniently be made, a space of some eight to thirteen feet, depending on the length of the tails of the roofing stones and the height of the vault. But the long axes of the build-

ing could be indefinitely prolonged. At first these houses seem to have been composed of three or four oblong rooms fitted together to form a rectangle. Later, when size began to be more esteemed, ranks of rooms were strung together like beads.

The highest development of this kind of building was found in Yucatan. Instead of a plaster façade, the facing of these houses was of stone, which was elaborately carved. The general field of decoration was between the top wall and the roof. Now a large building of several ranks of rooms was extremely unsatisfactory, since the inner rooms were deprived of light and air. To overcome this, the idea of creating second and third stories was

THE GREAT TEMPLE AT TENOCHTITLAN, THE ANCIENT MEXICO CITY

This building and that on page 27 show the Mexican emphasis on planes in contrast to the Maya use of ornament. The double temple is in honor of the Rain and War Gods. (See NATURAL HISTORY Volume XXXIII, pp. 18-19). Reconstruction by Ignacio Marquina

evolved. As we have seen in the temple architecture, it was incompatible with Maya idea of safety to support a great weight on a hollow foundation. In building a second story the Maya usually filled in the rooms immediately beneath the projected upper floor. To keep the maximum number of rooms in use, each of the rooms was stepped back from the one below. Another method of constructing an edifice of more than one story was to surround with ranks of rooms the platform supporting a building.

We have seen that at first the conception of an enclosed space was predominant, and that later air and light began to be considered by erecting several tiers of rooms. As a corollary of this, the simple doorway began to be split up into several portals, leading to an eventual evolution of the column. Toward the close of the Mexican occupation of Chichen Itza, the ranks of rooms so characteristic of Yucatan gave way to colonnades. Here wooden lintels strung from column to column carried the weight of the vaults.

HALL OF THE COLUMNS, MITLA, OAXACA

This is one of the largest completely walled buildings in Central America. Note the ingenious mosaic of separate blocks of stone. After Charnay and Viollet le Duc, 1862

TEMPLE AT XOCHICALCO, MORELOS

Another ornate example of Nahua architecture wherein the temple and platform are treated as a unit. The frieze falls into the Mixtec-Zapotec art style. After Totten, 1926

Perhaps because of accident of preservation, but more probably because of increased light, in buildings of this late period we begin to find interior ornament such as frescoes and carved and plastered columns. Unless designs could be seen, there would be no purpose in creating them, for the inner apartments of a simple collection of ranked rooms must have been almost pitch black.

The essential success of Maya architecture from the dramatic point of view was the invention of a monolithic type of construction involving the false arch, which rendered it possible to combine mass, height, and field for ornament, with inner space for the performance of cult practice. On the highlands of Mexico the basis of construction was much simpler. The false arch was unknown, and there was no such mastery of stone and concrete construction. Unfortunately, very few Mexican temples have been preserved.

In the first place, the people on the Mexican Highlands commonly used adobe and piled stone faced with cement, a type of construction that resists very poorly the destructive action of time. Instead of covering their buildings with corbel vaults, they erected flat roofs of plaster spread on beams, or pitched roofs of thatch or wood. Consequently we have no such obvious point of interest as in the miraculously preserved Maya buildings. However, one does have the impression that the effect of awe was gained by the vast, imposing mass of the substructure rather than the building on top.

Decorative treatment of the side walls of the platform was emphasized very rarely to the point of obscuring the central planes. While the most ornate frieze known from the Highland region is the deeply cut Temple of Quetzalcoatl at Teotihuacan, more often carvings like snakes' or death's-heads were inserted in

TEMPLE OF TAJIN, VERA CRUZ

As at Xochicalco (p. 31) the platform and temple are built as a unit. The apertures are small
niches for statues. This temple is most readily adaptable to European architectural ideas

the walls. The major ornament seems to have been the stair which was treated as a center of interest and not as a mere communication.

The plans of the temples were not so rigidly controlled by structural factors as in the Maya area. Roofs supported by wooden beams could cover wider spaces than stone slabs inched out to meet in a corbel vault. Under such circumstances an inner and an outer chamber of substantial size could be made. Sometimes the temples had stone walls and the roofs were lofty structures of wooden crib-work. A feature of many Aztec temples was the erection of two temples on a platform for whichever two gods in their pantheon were especially to be venerated. At Tenochtitlan there was a notable pair of shrines in honor of the Gods of War and Rain.

Palaces and priestly dwellings followed domestic architecture more closely. A number of rooms were grouped around courts, and colonnades were not uncommon. In some places, as at Teotihuacan, by using interior columns a large central room could be formed. Two-story houses are described in accounts of Mexico, but at the earlier site of Teotihuacan, our best source for priestly dwellings, platforms were used to elevate one room above another. As in the Maya area, there was the same mistrust of using the roof and walls of one room to support another.

A blending of Mexican and Mayan architectural ideas existed at Chichen Itza and at Tuloom. At Chichen Itza

CROSS SECTION OF A TEMPLE AT MITLA, OAXACA

(See p. 31 upper)

Compare this Mexican roof with the corbel vaults of the Maya (p. 26 lower). This structural method makes it possible to have wider rooms than under the Maya system. After Holmes, 1897

the Castillo showed a dramatic treatment of the substructure and stair, although the emphasis on the temple was in part Maya. More specifically the Temple of the Warriors resembled Mexico in the ornate friezes around the platform, and perhaps the use of the colonnade in the temple proper. However, the vaulting and general exterior treatment are Maya. At Tuloom we find an emphasis on mass and plane surfaces, as well as the flat roof of the Highlands. Conceivably this is the ultimate southeastern swing of the Mexican school of architecture.

These types of architecture, the Maya and the Mexican, express the two major styles of Central America. There are, however, certain other buildings which suggest the existence of different architectural evolutions.

Especially notable is the temple of Tajin near Papantla in Vera Cruz. In this case the temple was made one of the successive rising stages of the platform, thus creating a unified harmony between fane and substructure. There was no carving, although in niches set throughout the sides idols were placed; but these cannot have detracted from the essential unity of plane and mass. Another case where the temple was treated in terms of the platform was at Xochicalco. Here the planes of the building were subordinated as fields for an exquisitely carved relief, which suggested a Maya inspiration.

At Mitla, in Oaxaca, we have the three great "Palace" groups, each composed of oblong buildings on the three sides of a sunken court. The walls were ornamented

TULOOM, QUINTANA ROO, A FUSION OF MEXICO AND MAYA ARCHITECTURE. AFTER LOTHROP, 1924

with a mosaic of cut stones composing a lovely fretwork design. The flat roofs were partly supported by massive stone columns and include the largest completely walled floor spaces found in Central America.

This résumé has covered briefly the principal aspects of Central American architecture. Maya architecture emerged as triumphant glorification of design, as opposed to the Mexican emphasis on massive planes. Certain specialized buildings were mentioned which, although belonging to neither of these major styles, were none the less noteworthy. At the same time it must not be forgotten that Central America is spattered with mounds, the details of which are either irremediably destroyed or else have to be studied by excavation, so that only the broadest outlines of Central American architecture are visible to us.

THE TEMPLE OF THE WARRIORS, RECONSTRUCTED BY PROF. K. CONANT, AFTER MORRIS, 1931

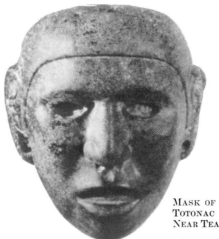

MASK OF GREEN STONE,
TOTONAC (?) CULTURE,
NEAR TEAYO, VERA CRUZ

The Sculpture of
Pre-Columbian Central America

The sculpture of Central America expresses in a more subtle and varied form the quality of impersonality noticeable in the architecture. The arts were created by nameless craftsmen to enrich their tribal ceremony, and were not expressions of the individual as they are today. Thus we see the Central American arts as a communal production, not the aesthetic reactions of a number of individual artists. Whereas the major buildings were the foci of the highly ceremonialized group religion, sculpture had a more diffuse function. Not only did it adorn the temples and explain their purpose but also it depicted the god honored within the shrine. Plastic forms were also utilized in the creation of incense burners and other temple furniture. Sculpture had its place in the life of the individual, who fashioned from various substances his household gods and votive offerings. Again, images of people and animals were sometimes made to put into graves as equipment for the next world.

If the plastic arts of the Central Americans were not entirely religious, their inspiration, at least, must have originated in ritualistic necessity, to judge from the all-permeating effect of religion on tribal life.

This religious domination makes Central American art seem to us cold, unsympathetic, and confused. Accustomed as we are to completely untrammeled artistic forms and to the glorification of the individual, it is hard for us to conceive how an art could be so imprisoned by ritual. Yet if we think back to the slow emergence of European art from the formulae of religious teaching, Central American sculpture becomes more conceivable. Its lack of emotional appeal is a question of racial interest. The Central Americans, to judge from their art, considered awe the proper emotional relation between the worshipper and his god. If European art had followed the Old Testament conceptions of religion instead of the New, the artistic forms of Europe and

"HOUSE OF THE NUNS," AT UXMAL, YUCATAN, MEXICO

Late Maya period. Detail of the inner façade. Note the conventionalization of the superimposed serpent masks. Here religious symbolism has all but obscured the direct visual image, but there is complete mastery of design. After Holmes, 1915

CENTRAL VERA CRUZ SCULPTURE

In this carving of a wild turkey, the requirements of design are met, although the presentation is naturalistic. To represent it more dramatically, the figure is shown base upward

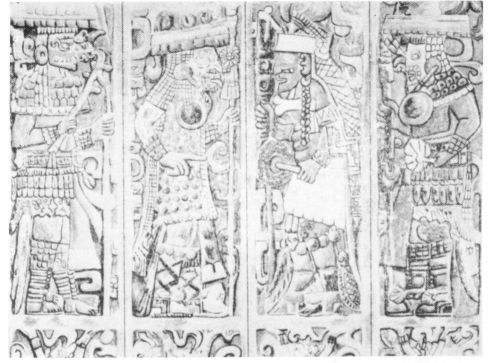

TEMPLE OF THE CHACMOOL, CHICHEN ITZA, YUCATAN

Period of Mexican influence. These pilaster figures represent a stage midway between the complete religious symbolism (page 36, upper) of the late Maya and the more naturalistic treatment of the Nahua peoples. After Morris, Charlot, and Morris, 1931

CLAY TIGER FROM OAXACA, MEXICO

Zapotec culture. A tiger god is represented by this clay figure. The attributes of divinity detract little from the lively realism of the figure proper which has been humanized to some extent

Central America might have produced a very similar emotional effect.

Another conflict between the modern observer and ancient American art is the variation in the ethnic ideal of beauty. Consequently, it is well to remember that the Central Americans were reproducing their own racial type.

The confused quality of the art arises from two factors, the presentation of the attributes and symbols of the various gods and the extreme fascination which complicated design held for the Central American. After all, if we examined medieval painting according to its original purpose instead of from our modern technical and aesthetic point of view, we would be infinitely bewildered trying to understand the attributes of the various individuals and the exact significance of the scene. Furthermore, simplicity or complexity in plastic design veers from one extreme to the other in the history of European art, so that Central American art cannot be justly dismissed by us on the ground of complexity alone. Therefore, if we discount our racial and emotional prejudices, aroused all too quickly by the unfamiliar, we find in Central American sculpture a competent and versatile art, well adapted to the portrayal of human beings, as well as the relationship between them and their gods.

This sculpture is known to us chiefly by examples in stone and clay. Because of their perishability, few carvings in wood have been found, and shell, owing to its size, was used only for the making of ornaments. The carving of semi-precious stones like jade we shall defer to a later article on jewelry.

The earliest sculptures found are small figurines of clay. Their evolution can be traced fairly accurately through ascending stages wherein experiment and variety alternate with conventionalization arising from the attainment of temporarily satisfactory forms. The human form engaged the attention of these

GUERRERO, MEXICO
Unknown culture. This head of a monkey in black stone presents a happy balance between design and reproduction of a living form

early sculptors and there was a sustained effort to give the little figurines vitality by countless experiments in depicting the features. Owing to the difficulty of supporting strips of wet clay, arms and legs had to be disposed in more or less passive positions so that little action could ever be shown. Usually there is an underlying stylistic unity between the plastic product of each tribe, but occasionally individual expression obtrudes.

In the early culture groups clay sculpture was the dominating artistic medium, and, seemingly, the religion in those days must have been a simple anthropomorphism. With the rise of civilization the art was transformed to meet the requirements of religion, and the clay sculpture was no longer a dominant plastic medium. The development of a pantheon composed of different divinities atrophied the simple naturalism of the earlier art, and the invention of the clay mould made it possible to cast myriads of figures scrupulously defined by their attributes. Thus the craftsman tended to abandon this mechanical reproduction of divinities and utilize stone as a medium of expression, although he occasionally worked in clay with the most harmonious results. Conceivably, the increased specialization of individual activity in a developed civilization allowed men the opportunity to dedicate themselves to religious art, and

OAXACA, MEXICO

Zapotec culture. This clay figure in the Oaxaca Museum is a striking example of Central American art, when allowed to express itself without religious symbolism. Photograph by Miguel Covarrubias

to utilize materials like stone, which required time to shape.

We know on archaeological grounds that stone sculpture developed later than clay in the Maya and the Mexican regions. While it began like the clay plastic, in the round, it took a somewhat different course. Where clay could be readily shaped, stone had to be laboriously pecked and ground into the desired form. On the basis of the earliest stone carvings recovered from Central American sites, there seems to have been no inheritance

COPAN, HONDURAS
Early Maya culture. One of the best examples of Maya sculpture is this magnificent limestone
head in the Peabody Museum. Compare it with the racial types shown on pages 35 and
39. This photograph and that on the opposite page are by Dr. Clarence Kennedy

COPAN, HONDURAS

Early Maya culture. This conventionalized serpent head, also in the Peabody Museum, expresses vividly the ceremonial preoccupation of the Central American sculptors, which all but extinguished their extraordinary naturalistic gifts, as exemplified on the opposite page

CUERNAVACA, MORELOS

Gualupita I culture. The genesis of the sculptor's art lay in the development of clay figurines like this in the Bourgeois collection in Mexico

from a former wood-carver's technique of which such strong traces exist in the sculpture of the archaic Greeks and ancient Egyptians. Wood-carving, on the contrary, appears to have followed in the path of the stone-work. Such a condition could well arise from the absence of adequate metal cutting tools, which so hampered the Central American sculptor.

It is perhaps owing to this circumstance that we note one of the most striking differences between Egypto-Grecian and Central American carving. The insistence in Old World art on anatomy would result from *hewing* out the rough outline of the figure, but the Central American preoccupation with external contour would arise from pecking and smoothing down the resistant stone surfaces. Probably the fleshy physical type of the Central American, in contrast to the

muscular and bony European, also contributed to this divergence in presentation.

Once the Central American sculptors had mastered their material sufficiently to fulfill their conceptions of gods, men, and animals, they began to develop the various applications of sculpture and also to establish regional styles. Even as in architecture, there is discernible the cleavage between the gentle Maya and the fierce Highland tribes like the Nahuas and the Zapotecs.

Maya sculpture in stone is chiefly to be found enriching buildings or composing those great monoliths on which the priests caused to be inscribed the ceremonial pattern of their calendar. But scarcely a specimen exists of complete sculpture in the round, such as might be enthroned on the central altar of a temple to symbolize a god.

CUERNAVACA, MORELOS

Gualupita II culture. This clay figure represents an advance over the crude work of the preceding period. It is but a short step from this figure to the skilful presentation on page 39

The most impressive sculpture comes from Copan, Honduras, where exquisitely carved figures ornamented an architecture that, compared to other Maya cities, was inferior. Great skill was shown in bringing out the soft outlines of human faces, and, in the depiction of bodies, real anatomical skill was displayed. Grotesque beings were conceived with equal imagination and artistry. The great stone blocks of the stelae or time markers also presented majestic figures, carved in such deep relief that only the back of the block, containing the inscription, disqualified them from being sculpture in the round. To the north at Quirigua this art reached its zenith in gigantic stelae, twenty-five feet high, and in those fantastic boulders, ornamented and reornamented into an essence of ceremonial involution.

To the west, across the lowlands of

PUEBLA, MEXICO
Unknown culture. This simple and vigorous presentation of a Highland face is characteristic of Nahua stonework. The eyes were probably inlaid with shell and obsidian

Guatemala, is another style of Maya sculpture, that of the cities of the Usumacintla River. Here, at Yaxchilan and Piedras Negras, lintels of hard zapote wood or of limestone were adorned by scenes in low relief. Stelae, too, were decorated in the same manner, and, although some of the relief is very deep, nowhere does it approach sculpture in the round. The finest examples of this school come from downstream, at Palenque. So low is the relief and so firm the line, that the sculpture almost enters into the realm of drawing and painting. Especially interesting in this Usumacintla art is the naturalistic treatment of the figures which are framed by the hieroglyphic text.

To the north, in Yucatan, the sculptures are largely reduced to theological abstractions, wherein the gods are depicted by a harmonious disposal of their

TEOTIHUACAN, MEXICO
Teotihuacan culture. This crude figure more than ten feet high represents an early stage in stone carving, which seems not to have been developed until long after modeling in clay

PIEDRAS NEGRAS, PETEN DISTRICT, GUATEMALA

Maya culture. One of the loveliest Maya treatments of life forms is this detail from a door lintel. Comparing it with the relief on the opposite page, one can see the difficulty in using modern European aesthetics to choose the best examples of an art based on totally different canons. Photograph by Dr. Clarence Kennedy

PANTALEON, GUATEMALA

Pipil (?) culture. This detail from a massive carving seems to represent a blending of Maya artistic formulæ with the rugged strength of the Highland sculpture. Little is known of the ethnic affiliations of this distinctive school of stone carving

COSTA RICA

Guetar culture. This almost life-size stone figure comes from one of the cultures peripheral to the great Central American civilizations. It has a crude vigor, unobscured by the detail of religious symbolism

attributes. Such treatment precludes an appreciation of this carving as true sculpture, since it is, in reality, pure design. With the intrusion of the Mexicans and the rise of Chichen Itza, naturalistic reliefs again found favor, but they also had a strong theological flavor in their involved ornament.

Bordering on the Maya area to the south in Costa Rica and Nicaragua is a sculpture that represents a stylistic midpoint between the civilized conceptions of the Maya and the somewhat fumbling naturalism of the early cultures. Although probably contemporaneous with the best art of the Maya, it shows the archaism of provincial districts. There is, however, a rugged boldness about the major sculptures that establishes

them as highly significant forms.

The sculpture of the Mexican Highland at the outset seems to have fallen under rigid theological control. The sculptures at San Juan Teotihuacan and the grotesque divinities of the later Aztecs reflect the elements of pure design arising from the theological use of form. Yet occasionally one finds superb naturalistic treatment of divine subjects. Nowhere on the Central Plateau does that balance between the intrinsic beauty of natural forms and the harmonious design of theological conception obtain as in the Maya sculptures of Copan and the Usumacintla region. However, the art of this people freshly endowed with the paraphernalia of civilization has an undoubted strength and vigor that one does not feel in the gradual unfolding of the older and softer Maya civilization.

This conflict in Aztec art between the grotesque conventionalization of religious dogma and the naturalism arising from increased skill in portraying human forms may be seen reduced to its essential constituents in the arts of the Zapotec and the Totonac. The Zapotec of Oaxaca practised an extremely formalized art best exemplified in their clay funerary urns. In these specimens ritual is apparent in every line. Clay models were used to build up the ornaments and attributes of the divinities portrayed. Human or animal forms were used as a terrifying background for the addition of ceremonial features. Yet excellent naturalistic sculptures occur scattered infrequently through this art.

Among the Totonac of Vera Cruz we find the reverse, that the conventionalization of religious formulae is subordinated to a rich portrayal of the human form.

Whenever conventionalization is deemed necessary, it is concentrated on some object like a ceremonial yoke, but it is nowhere used to throttle a naturalistic expression. Extremely entertaining are the clay "laughing heads," which grin with a blissful good humor. A number of the heads from the Totonac region were shown with oblique eyes, and created the belief in some quarters that this was Chinese influence. Since the American Indian is of Mongoloid stock, it is not surprising that such traits as the epicanthic fold should be reproduced in the sculpture, but it by no means implies that Chinese art had any connection with Central American.

From the point of view of the European, these east coast Mexican forms are the most satisfying of all the various Central American sculptures, since there is a minimum of theological grotesqueness. Closely connected with this Totonac art is that of the Huaxtecs at the north of

TEMPOAL, VERA CRUZ, MEXICO
Huaxtec culture. This seated female figure is a survival of the most primitive art in clay

Vera Cruz. Although Maya-speaking, their sculpture shows no artistic influence from the parent stock and is noteworthy in its appreciation of youth.

An exquisite group of sculptures comes from a strip of territory that runs from coast to coast between the lands of the Aztecs and the Zapotecs. Conjecture might attribute these marvellous carvings to the Olmec, who appear in the dim background of mythological history. It is a perplexing paradox that the creators of the beautiful heads and ornaments from this area, which were traded far and wide, must rest in anonymity, unless further research can define them. Much of the sculpture belongs to the lapidary's art.

Another important style of sculpture comes from the Pacific slopes of Guatemala and expresses a fusion of Nahua vigor and Maya mastery of ritualistic design. This plastic style suggests a sudden genesis, rather than the slow evolution of a self-contained tribal art.

Finally, the rich clay plastic of Western Mexico gives us an idea of the utmost

GUIAROO, OAXACA, MEXICO
Zapotec (?) culture. The rugged racial type of the Mexican Highlands is shown vividly by this small stone head

development of a people who were subjected neither to the discipline of complicated ritual nor to the stimulation of a highly organized religion. While there is great variety in subject and attitudes, the characteristic one would expect from an art in the hands of the people, there is none of the finish of the Central American arts under hierarchical control. If these western Mexican sculptures are basically religious and intended for use as mortuary offerings, they are nevertheless worked out by lay methods. They are in reality survivals of an older aesthetic system.

However unified the purpose of Central American sculpture, it is not the product of a single people and should not be so considered. It is the product of a number of tribal groups, of different language and physical types, striving to glorify their religion, according to their various abilities. Yet there is, none the less, a generic resemblance in the sculpture as a

QUIRIGUA, GUATEMALA, MAYA CULTURE. THIS STELE OR TIME-MARKER IS SOME 25 FEET HIGH AND SHOWS THE CEREMONIAL ART OF THE MAYA AT ITS BEST. AFTER MAUDSLAY, 1889-1902

whole, which lies in the absence of those sensual and emotional features that characterize our own. It is not to be expected that people of one race can derive from the art of another the same psychological reaction, particularly if it is religious. However, the detached and impersonal repose of the Central American sculptures has a soothing effect in this modern era where intensely independent individuals strive to perpetuate their personalities in the face of mass production. While there is conflict in Central American sculptures between the freedom necessary for naturalism and the conventionalization dictated by theology, it is a struggle of technique. The creators of the sculptures were harmonizing their tribal life with the rhythms of nature. They expressed their gratitude for divine favors through the skilled anonymity of their craftsmen, and their works registered complete content without a sign of the fickle protest in our modern art.

WESTERN MEXICO. THESE CLAY FIGURES EXEMPLIFY THE VITALITY AND HUMOR OF A FOLK ART UNAFFECTED BY REQUIREMENTS OF RITUAL

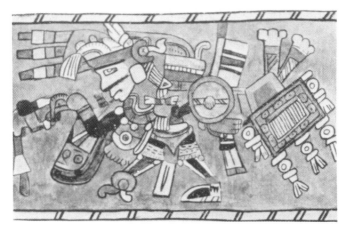

Fresco, Tizatlan, Tlaxcala, Mexico. After Caso, 1927

The Art of Painting in Pre-Columbian Central America

CENTRAL American painting does not show the same masterly control over subject and material that is so evident in the architecture and sculpture. Perhaps this inferiority may be due to the rarity of examples. Frescos and deerskin or paper manuscripts are extremely perishable, so that few specimens have survived the action of the weather or the destructive fanaticism of the Spanish priesthood. Much more probably, however, the ritualistic restrictions which controlled the architecture and sculpture have limited painting even more, for this art was confined to a didactic or explanatory supplement to the religious symbolism expressed by the stone carving, or else was used for simple narrative purposes in connection with the historical annals.

The term "painting" we are using in the common sense of the word, to mean a picture, not the mere laying on of colors. Hence we shall not consider the designs on pottery vessels nor touch on the coloring of sculpture, which was a universal Central American practice. On the border line of this subject are the low reliefs of Chichen Itza and the Usumacintla River sites. These sculptured friezes were coated and corrected with plaster before they were painted, but they do not really fall within the scope of *painting and draughtsmanship*. Therefore we shall confine ourselves to the examples of frescos, manuscripts, and vases which depict actual scenes, in distinction to designs.

Few frescos have survived, since those natural agencies which have caused whole buildings to crumble, attack first the paintings on their walls. The surviving examples display colors such as red, blue, yellow, and green, obtained from ochreous earths and sometimes from vegetable dyes. Occasionally scarlet cochineal, obtained from insects, was employed. The earliest examples known to us are from San Juan Teotihuacan in the Highlands of Mexico, where the painter, despite

Caracol,
Chichen Itza,
Yucatan

This circular astronomical observatory is shown partly restored by the Carnegie Institution of Washington. The disintegration by natural forces that ruins massive buildings like this offers scant chance of survival to perishable materials like frescos and manuscripts. The wonder of Central American painting is that any examples survived at all

This limestone low relief from Tabasco illustrates the transition between drawing and sculpture. The Central American never could suggest by his brush the delicate contours he achieved in modeling

The painter of the vase from Guatemala, a detail of which is shown below, lacked only an accurate knowledge of perspective to equal the masterly result of the sculptor whose work is shown above. After Gordon, 1925-28

his rude drawing, has caught in lively terms a ceremonial scene. Especially noteworthy is a conventionalized design combining various fruits and plants.

Most of the frescos presumably date from the time immediately preceding the Conquest, and come from Yucatan where the rugged stone architecture resisted the elements, and in consequence preserved the fragile paintings within the rooms of the buildings. A number of the subjects seem to be secular. At the Temple of the Warriors, in Chichen Itza, two animated scenes were reconstructed by Ann Axtell Morris from the fallen blocks of the temple vault. In one a seaside village is shown, and in the other the defeat of a foray by marauding strangers. There is no real grasp of foreshortening, but the arrangement of the figures suggests a dawning knowledge of perspective. In the Temple of the Tigers at the same site there is a fresco depicting another attack, and in this case some rather successful attempts at foreshortening have been achieved. At other sites like Chacmultun scenes have been attempted but the draughtsmanship is crude.

Religious Frescos

There are a number of purely religious frescos, without the secular element introduced by the presence of human beings. The most celebrated are found at Santa Rita in northern British Honduras and at Tuloom on the east coast of Yucatan. In this group the element of design is dominant, and the divinities are arranged according to the dictates of ceremonial pattern. Curiously enough, although found in Maya territory, these frescos have strong affinities in subject and style to the paintings at Mitla in distant Oaxaca.

The Mitla frescos are entirely ceremonial, being composed of divinities and their attributes, and they are closely related to the codices or ritualistic books of that area. Other Oaxacan examples are extremely rare, and in Central Mexico, save for the frescos at Teotihuacan already mentioned, the painted altars at Tizatlan, near Tlaxcala, alone are worth consideration. These designs are composed in brilliant colors, but the content is purely ritualistic and ceremonial. Like the Mitla frescos, the draughtsmanship is closely related to that of the manuscripts.

Illuminated Manuscripts

By one of those constant paradoxes in Central America, codices abound where frescos are few, and vice-versa. Thus on the Mexican Highlands there are many illuminated manuscripts, but, as we have seen, few frescos have survived. On the other hand, in the Maya country, the source of most of our knowledge of fresco painting, only three books have been preserved. For a knowledge of draughtsmanship, the manuscripts are a most valuable source of information. They include ritualistic and divinatory manuals, historical annals, tribute rolls, maps, and the like. Thus in the rendition of the subjects chosen, artistic considerations were always secondary to the needs of exposition.

Middle American writing was at a relatively primitive stage. It was ideographic and phonetic, the principle being that of our modern rebus. There was, however, no means of conjugating verbs or declining nouns. Consequently action had to be expressed by pictures. It is quite probable that long recitations learned by rote and passed on from generation to generation supplemented the picture writings which served as a mnemonic aid. A great many of these documents gave calendric and astronomical calculations, and the inscriptions are largely composed of the names and numbers of the various dates, the pictures of the gods presiding over the various days, and the ceremonies associated with them.

Painted Relief from Chichen Itza

This carved wall from the lower chamber, Jaguar Temple, was covered with plaster and then painted. A procession of priests and warriors converges on an altar in honor of their god Quetzalcoatl, the Feathered Serpent. The warriors carry spears and spear-throwers, and the two priests have feathered robes in their hands

Ritualistic uses of painting. The upper picture, an altar at Teotihuacan (Gamio, 1922), shows religious formulae reduced to pure design. The middle picture from the Codex Florentino describes a ceremony in which people dressed as birds or gods participate. At the bottom is a scene from the Vienna Codex after Humboldt, 1814. The content is partly ceremonial and partly historic

Descriptive uses of painting include this woodland scene from the Temple of the Warriors at Chichen Itza. The panther in the tree suggests that the artist cared more about defining his genera than drawing them naturally. After Maudslay, 1889-1902

Detail from a battle scene, Temple of the Warriors, Chichen Itza, shows considerable animation in the house to house fighting and the captives being led off for sacrifice by the black-painted priests. After Morris, Charlot and Morris, 1931

Tikal

This dramatic model constructed by Herbert Maier, aided by H. Marchand and H. B. Wright, for the Buffalo Museum shows a typical early Maya ceremonial center. The jungle has wreaked havoc with the site so that now little except the architecture remains of the achievements of its builders. Thus the incomplete patchwork comprising present knowledge of Central America utilizes scraps from many sources

Perishable remains like this plaster temple at Uaxactun, Peten District, Guatemala, are sometimes miraculously preserved. This model cross-section shows how a later building sheathed the earlier structure and protected it (See p. 21)

This fresco from Teotihuacan, perhaps the earliest in this series, was saved in the same way. Men and women offer gifts to the statues of two gods at either side of the picture. On the altars before them burn sacred fires. After Gamio, 1922

The three Maya books fall into this last category. As the Maya had developed an extremely conventionalized way of depicting word symbols, the pages, from an artistic point of view, do not compare with the Highland documents. Among the latter the manuscripts assignable to the Mixtec civilization are especially handsome. The day signs and the representations of the divinities are carefully, one might say arduously, drawn. Proportions are based upon the ritualistic importance of the details shown rather than their anatomical symmetry. Colors are used not only to reproduce natural tones but also to define the object ceremonially, since colors had a strong ritualistic significance in Central American religion. Permeating all the symbols, and their distribution on the page, is design, which follows closely in the train of the order implicit in ritual.

AZTEC PAINTING

In comparison to the Mixtec documents, the painting in Aztec manuscripts seems barbaric, but because it is less confined by ceremonial restrictions it has a freshness rather engaging to our eyes. Furthermore, the Aztec system of writing was incorporated into the Spanish colonial administration, both as a method for keeping legal records pertaining to Indian affairs and as a means for disseminating Christianity among the natives. It is, therefore, possible to see in a number of drawings the transition from a purely Indian to quasi-European style of draughtsmanship.

In the purely ceremonial documents, like the *tonalamatl* or sacred almanac, there was a close connection with the extremely stylized documents of the south, but there is more immediate interest to the casual reader in the annals. These follow two forms. One is in the nature of a map, where the events are set forth much as are localities. A knowledge of the symbols defining personages and tribes does not explain the action entirely, so that manuscripts of this type must have been supplements to oral tradition. The other class is more self-contained. The symbols for the years were set down successively, and lines connect the various events pictured with the year glyphs. Some of these records, like the *Annals of 1576,* were kept well into Colonial times, but the text gradually shifted from picture-writing to Nahuatl words transliterated into Spanish characters.

Another category of documents is composed of the tribute rolls, land grants, and similar administrative records. The Aztecs kept careful account of the toll to be exacted from the towns they conquered. Pictures of the objects with symbols for the quantity are set down together with the hieroglyphs designating the tributary pueblos. Other records show the land held by individuals and the rent payable, and, as these records were retained in colonial times, there is often a gloss in European characters, describing in Spanish or Nahuatl the significance of the document. A few colonial manuscripts exist wherein the symbols were rearranged into a sort of phonetic writing, suitable to record prayers. The Spanish priests broke down the ideographs into a system of actual writing, but the greater serviceability of Spanish characters caused this attempt soon to be abandoned.

CODEX FLORENTINO

The most diverting document from Central America is the Codex Florentino, a collection of pictures illustrating Father Bernardino Sahagun's exhaustive work, *A General History of the Things of New Spain,* written about 1565. These drawings depict every detail of Aztec social life and religion, not to speak of delightful excursions into natural history. The draughtsmanship suggests the phrase

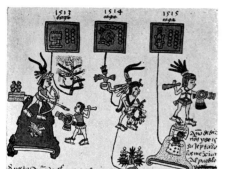

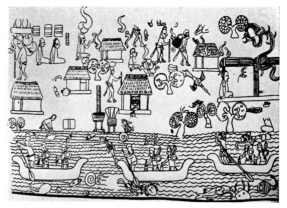

Mexican narrative painting. Successively presented are the Conquests of Montezuma II (*Codex Telleriano-Remensis*), a seashore in Yucatan (*Temple of the Warriors*), the meeting of Cortes and Montezuma (*Lienzo de Tlaxcala*), the migration of the Nahua tribes (*Codex Boturini*), an Aztec ceremony, (*Codex Borbonicus*), and an Aztec tribute roll (*Tribute Roll of Montezuma*)

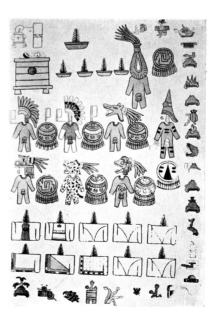

This mortuary bowl from Uaxactun shows great ease and freedom in drawing. The hole in the center of the vessel was made to kill the pot, so that it could pass with its owner to the next world. After Smith, 1932

The detail shown below from another Maya vase commemorates the meeting between a Maya chief (at the left) and a noble stranger. The features are accentuated to express racial differences. The glyphs doubtless give explanatory details. After Dieseldorff, 1904

This painting from a Mixtec history, the Codex Nuttall, involves a group of warriors in canoes, who are attacking a town on an island in a lake. Note the ingeniously stylized wild life which inhabits the water. After Joyce, 1927

No such schematic drawings as shown above mar this Maya vase from Copan, which represents a quetzal or trogon, the sacred bird of the Maya. After Gordon, 1928

"old wine in new bottles," since despite the influence of European methods of drawing, the content and psychology are Aztec.

The preceding pages have outlined the two principal sources for Central American painting, the frescos and the manuscripts. While the frescos show a certain fresh ability in presentation, the manuscripts on the whole exhibit the lifelessness that one would expect from the standardized repetition of signs and symbols already defined by ritual. The draughtsmanship does not equal the sculpture and the architecture. Yet there is the inevitable exception to every generalization, and this is to be found in a small group of Maya vases, where a lively and subtle style of drawing is to be found.

Human figures, naturalistically presented, are extremely rare in Central American pottery decoration, and are confined almost exclusively to the Maya region. The style commences at Copan in a vigorous shorthand and finally blossoms into its fullest flower in the Chama region of Guatemala, although there seems to have been a sub-center in the Peten district of the same country.

The scenes are apparently purely descriptive. A notable receiving an embassy from another tribe is depicted on one vase. On another a high personage is borne on a litter, and a third vessel is decorated by a scene wherein a chief

seated on a throne holds a levee. The racial types are exaggerated, but the positions of the body are as graceful in carriage as they are harmonious in design. The strong, sure outlines recall the best of the low reliefs from the Usumacintla River region, and it is apparent that the same school of draughtsmanship which inspired the vase painting controlled also the outlines of the reliefs. When we remember that sculpture was always painted in Central America, it will be seen that here painting and sculpture blend. In the Maya vase painting we have at last found an approximation to the beauties of the stone carving.

The art of painting in Central America exists for us by implication, much as does the delineative art of the ancient Greeks for which vase painting and literary description are the principal sources since the paintings themselves have disappeared.

The frescos are not really representative, because either, as in the case of the Teotihuacan examples, they came from a primitive civilization, or, as in the Yucatan, they were the product of a decadent one. In the codices, the draughtsman's skill, because of delineative and ritualistic conventions, had no opportunity to express itself save in design. Only in Mayan vase painting do we find that the painters give indications of a skill equal to that of the architects and the sculptors.

Maya vase, from Nebaj, Guatemala. After Gordon, 1928

The Crafts of
Pre-Columbian Central America

MANY of the crafts of ancient Central America have persisted to the present day in spite of the transformations which the Spanish Colonial Empire and modern industry have wrought on the native civilizations. The major arts of the ancient peoples now exist more as an heirloom than a useful heritage. The modern artists from the Central American republics have recently utilized aboriginal themes, but between them and their source material stretch four hundred years of European artistic inspiration. In the crafts, however, there are connections, ofttimes tenuous to be sure, with the aboriginal industries. Sometimes only the technique survives, and the subject matter is completely Spanish Colonial or modern Republican. None the less, it is in the crafts that we feel most strongly the influence of the Indian past.

The applied arts of the ancient civilizations embodied many of those characteristics noted in architecture, sculpture, and painting. The same religious purpose that dominated the stone carving not only extended to ceremonial dress and temple paraphernalia, but even penetrated into secular possessions. Thus the elaborate decorative expression of ceremonial values influenced the craftsman as much as it did the creator of artistic masterpieces. Such a result, however, is natural, for there are no sharply drawn distinctions between the two spheres of action. Skilful workers were drafted to enhance the religious ceremonial, which gave the chief outlet for aesthetic expression. Wealth and social position, which make possible the private possession of fine things, were inextricably combined with the gradations of the religious hierarchy.

Surviving examples of these ancient arts must often take the place of selected masterpieces, for most of the perishable material has disappeared, owing to natural decay or to the willful destruction of war and conquest. Often the written descriptions of the Spanish Conquerors or the crabbed drawings in the native documents offer the sole testimony of remarkable craftsmanship in ancient Central America. Descriptions of the jewelry and pottery we shall reserve for succeeding chapters, since much of this material is wrought of imperishable substances and has survived in far greater quantities than examples of weaving, featherwork, wood carving, and the like.

Weaving was an important art in Central America, but few examples have resisted decay. To determine its degree of excellence we must rely on knowledge derived from other areas, where arid climates have preserved textiles and other perishable materials. The Basket Makers of the Southwestern United States, the earliest agriculturists discovered in that region, developed great skill in weaving cloths, sandals, and baskets, before they learned how to make pottery. Thus we can postulate with some confidence that weaving in the New World was well advanced on a very early cultural horizon. At the other extreme we find the magnificent textile art of ancient Peru, miraculously available to posterity, because the arid climate preserved thousands of burials, each enveloped in several lovely fabrics. That distinguished authority, Mr. M. D. C. Crawford, said of Peruvian weaving, "No single people we know ever invented and perfected so many forms of textiles," and again, "In tapestry Peru reached its highest textile development. The harmony of color, the beauty and the fastness of the dyes, and the perfection of

Costumes

The richness of Aztec costume deeply impressed the Spanish Conquistadores, but the contemporary drawings do scant justice to the originals. These illustrations by Keith Henderson for Prescott's *Conquest of Mexico*, published by Henry Holt in 1922, recapture the splendor of the Aztec scene, thanks to the artist's study of native source material

This drawing of the Aztec ambassadors to Cortes shows the dress of high officials. Note the elaborate coiffure and the ornamental mantles. The feather fans further add to the splendor of the costumes

This procession of warriors shows the imagination that governed gala dress. As this is a peace-time occasion, they are carrying flowers and standards in the place of weapons. Cotton, skins, feathers, and paper were utilized in composing these outfits

Women's dress, as exemplified by these Totonac girls, was relatively simple, yet with a little tailoring these lovely fabrics would not be out of place as sports costumes today

spinning and weaving, place these fabrics in a class by themselves, not only as compared to other textiles of this land, but as regards those of any other people."

Although we have scant means of judging the relative merits of the fabrics of Central America and Peru on the basis of weaving technique, we can compare their designs. The Mexican tribute rolls list mantles in many patterns, and on the great Maya sculptures we see evidence of the most elaborately decorated vestments. These designs are by no means inferior to those adorning the textiles of Peru. If the actual weaving processes were less developed in Central America than in Peru, the decorative aspects must have been very nearly equal.

ENRICHMENT OF FABRICS

The greatest development of the Central American textile art lay in dress. Although the quality of the garments depended on the station of the wearer, the basic costume was the same for all classes. Men wore a breech clout and mantle, knotted at the neck, both made of cotton or maguey fiber. Women usually were clothed in a skirt and a long blouse, the *huipil* which is still worn in parts of Central America. Such costumes could be varied or enriched by the quality of the fabric or by its decoration of brocade, openwork patterns, or embroidery. Additional means of enriching the fabrics were provided by tie-dyeing, batik, and complete dyeing in colors made of various vegetable and animal substances like logwood or cochineal. Clay stamps were used to print designs either on the fabrics or on the skins of the wearers.

The accessories of dress called into play much cunning craftsmanship, since for ceremonial occasions and warfare dazzling costume was demanded. A conspicuous element of ceremonial dress involved the use of feathers. Sometimes the feathers were attached to a loosely woven fabric in such a way that they made an actual cloth, with the designs worked out in various colors. The plumage of different birds was also employed as a mosaic adorning shields and helmets. Long plumes of tropical birds furnished crests on headgear or formed part of the standards which picked warriors wore on their backs to distinguish various clan and tribal units.

FEATHERWORK AND WOOD CARVING

Today the finer types of weaving and featherwork have disappeared with the destruction of the ancient religion, and the adoption of European costumes for gala occasions. An attractive embroidery still lingers on the Highlands of Guatemala, although many European motives have entered the designs. The featherwork, too, has almost ceased to exist, but, during the Colonial and early Republican period in Mexico, a sort of landscape painting in feather inlay survived.

Wood carving, like weaving, would be difficult to appraise, had not a number of examples found their way to Europe as trophies of the Conquest. Other specimens have either been guarded as heirlooms, or discovered by chance in dry caves. Prof. M. H. Saville, in his *Wood Carvers' Art in Ancient Mexico,* has gathered together all the available information on this art. The most intricate work is represented on several atlatls or throwing sticks, which must have been reserved for state occasions. The same mastery of design which distinguishes the major works of art characterizes this carving. Wooden drums show equal artistic ability and the human and animal forms of several belong properly to the realm of sculpture. The construction of one type, the *teponaztli,* required considerable ability, for the sounding board consisted of two tongues of wood which were partly freed from the hollowed block of the drum and gave different notes. Although the tone of the drums varied considerably, the interval between the notes of each was always the same.

MOSAIC WORK

Masks of wood for religious purposes were frequently made, since the gods were im-

Turquoise mosaic mirror, Chichen Itza, Yucatan. The reflecting surface was probably made of a number of fragments of iron pyrites laid against the sandstone center. The elaborateness of the setting together with its discovery beneath an altar indicates that its use was ritualistic. After Morris, Charlot and Morris, 1931

Right:—Obsidian mirror with gilded wooden frame, Mexico. This exceedingly rare specimen was purchased in Europe and may well have been among the presents sent to Charles V by Cortes

Lacquer tray. These gay utensils were a characteristic product of Mexican Indians during the Colonial period, and in recent years their manufacture has been revived in various villages in western Mexico. It is probable that their origin is Pre-Columbian

Rich Man

The Codex Florentino consists of several hundred paintings by Aztec artists to illustrate Father Sahagun's great work on the Aztec civilization. The pictures shown here give an idea of the complexity of the civilization. Besides the divisions expressed by our nursery rhyme, "Rich man, poor man,—" there was a great variety of other trades and professions, some of which

Poor Man

Gold Worker

Beggar Man

Feather Worker

Thief

Soldiers

Mexican Album

are shown at the bottom of these pages. Since the illustrations were intended for secular consumption, naïve vivacity (see "Bathers") replaces the usual ritualistic formality. Compare these drawings with those of Keith Henderson on pages 64-65, to see how faithfully that artist caught the native spirit, and to guide the eye in perceiving the subject matter which is depicted in this group

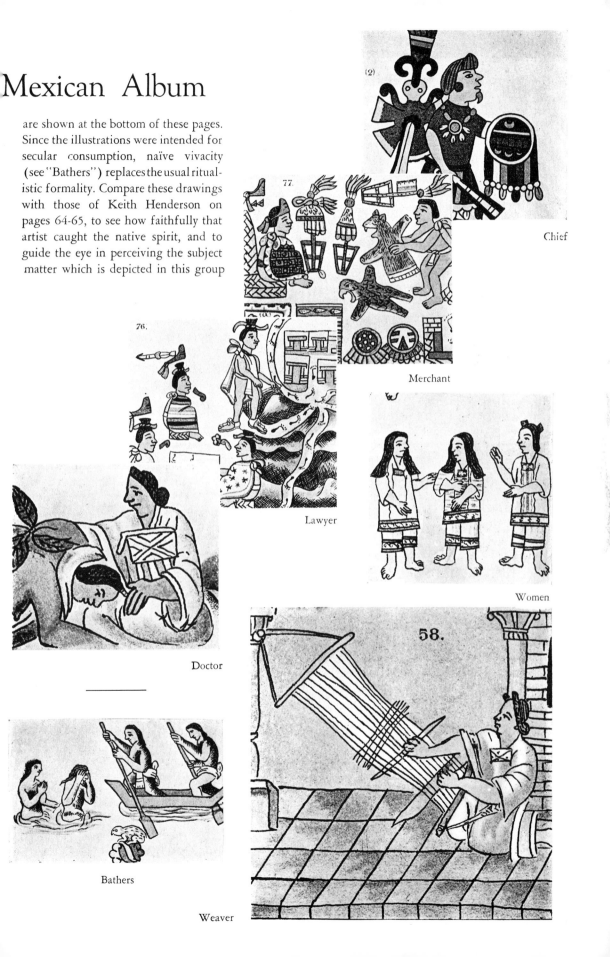

Chief

Merchant

Lawyer

Women

Doctor

Bathers

Weaver

personated in a number of ceremonies. Warfare, too, created a function for the wood carver in providing helmets which frequently took the form of animal heads. Yet such work was really the base for another distinctive Mexican craft, mosaic work, for knowledge of which we are again indebted to the erudition of Professor Saville. Fragments of turquoise, jade, obsidian, and shell were inlaid with consummate skill, and this art was a favorite method of embellishing a multitude of implements and jewelry. One of the most extraordinary examples of the craft is a shield in the Museum of the American Indian, where a scene in low relief is carried out in turquoise mosaic. The temples at Mitla show an adaptation of this mosaic technique in the creation of decorative friezes. Today, however, little or nothing survives of this industry.

A craft much more widely practised was the cutting of shell. The demand for this easily manufactured substance was enormous. Few indeed were the New World peoples, however primitive and however distant from the coast, who did not barter for their quota. Shell most frequently was made into beads or pendants, and perhaps because of its almost universal use, seldom received the attention of the more skilful craftsmen. Yet conch shells were sometimes ground and carved into handsome trumpets, while some were covered with plaster and painted with ritualistic designs. A few engraved gorgets show how readily this material responded to a skilled craftsman, but such ornaments are rare. Evidence exists that the carapaces of turtles and armadillos were also worked in ancient times. Some very beautiful objects are made of tortoise shell, today, but it is problematical whether this can be called a legitimate survival, or is of European introduction. Far to the south, in Panama, there occur splendid bone carvings that are reminiscent of major sculptures. Mention should also be made of carved whale teeth in the same region, and carved jaguar fangs in the Maya country, a type of work which

showed considerable ingenuity in adapting the design to the natural form.

Horn and bone were substances perhaps too work-a-day for the highly skilled artisan. Needles, awls, flakers for stone tools, and many other household implements were made of bone, but seldom does one find a beautifully worked example. The most notable exceptions are the jaguar bones from the priestly tomb at Monte Alban. These were split and polished, and on their convex surfaces inscriptions of a ceremonial character were chased, with a minute precision worthy of the Japanese. The backgrounds of these patterns were picked out in turquoise mosaic. Engraved human femora, sometimes ornamented in mosaic, are grim reminders of the exigencies of Nahua religion.

STONE ARTIFACTS

Work in stone we have considered in respect to architecture and sculpture, and shall describe again in connection with jewelry. Yet to manufacture the ordinary implements of everyday life required a consummate mastery of an obdurate material. To detach in a single effort the thin blades of obsidian used as razors and scalpels for ceremonial blood letting necessitated as skilful a coördination of strength and skill as did the patient flaking of the great leaf-shaped sacrificial knives. Some of the axes ground from hard stones like jade and serpentine are aesthetically satisfying in their useful symmetry. This same pride in craftsmanship, which was not unlike that of a medieval smith, seems to have dominated even the manufacture of an arrowhead every facet of which shows the skilled impress of the worker's hand.

ANCIENT MIRRORS

The manufacture of mirrors gives yet another aspect of Central American capability. There were in that region relatively few substances that could take a polish high enough to give a reflection. Glass and bronze were unknown, and copper never seems to

Mosaic

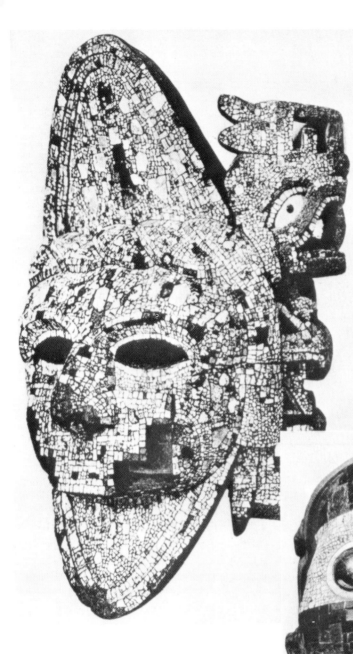

Mosaic working was one of the most elegant of Central American crafts, and color reproductions alone can give its true value. The wooden mask (taken like the two other illustrations on this page from Saville, 1922) was purchased from Cosimo de Medici for the Prehistoric and Ethnographic Museum in Rome, for two and one half francs. It must have been part of the loot from the conquest

Right:—This mosaic has as its matrix a human skull cut away in back to form a mask. It is one of the treasures of the British Museum. The lighter bands are turquoise and the darker, lignite

Left:—This sacrificial knife in the British Museum is a little more than a foot long. Turquoise, malachite, and variously colored shells compose the mosaic work which depicts an Eagle Knight

Featherwork is so extremely perishable that almost no Pre-Columbian examples survive. Under Spanish colonial influence, a sort of genre painting in feathers was developed which continued in Mexico until the middle of the last century. Examples of this feather painting in its degenerate state are shown at the left and on the opposite page. At the bottom of page 68 is shown a featherworker practising his craft, and from the pictures on pages 64 and 65 one can judge how important an adjunct to costume feathers were

This headdress (from Heger, 1908) originally belonged to the ill-fated Montezuma and was sent by Cortes to the Emperor Charles V, who in turn gave it to his nephew Ferdinand II of Tyrol. Kept in Ferdinand's castle at Ambras, this unique headdress finally became part of the collections of the Natural History Museum in Vienna

Feather-Work

The patient selection of different colored feathers and the care in joining them, as exemplified by this picture, made during the last century, is a direct expression of the Indian heritage in Mexico. It is curious to see in comparing this and the feather painting opposite with the costumes on pages 64 and 65 how little the dress of the Indian has changed with the ages. Only the trousers and the hat distinguish these people of 1850 from their ancestors of three centuries and a half before

have been used for such a purpose. The inhabitants did, however, make mirrors of iron pyrites and obsidian. Iron pyrites sometimes occur in small nodules on which a plane surface could be ground, giving a very satisfactory reflection. Another type of mirror consisted of thin plates of pyrites, laid like a mosaic on a backing of pottery or stone. Few complete specimens are known, but there do exist a number of stone discs which may well have been backs for such mirrors. It is quite probable that the celebrated mosaic disc from Chichen Itza could have had a mosaic of iron pyrites in its center. A unique mirror in the American Museum of Natural History utilizes iron pyrites in their original slate matrix, the pyrites being polished as a surface and the slate carved as an ornamental back. The obsidian mirrors of Central Mexico are among the wonders of ancient technology, since even a modern lapidary, with his diamond drills and carborundum wheels, has difficulty in grinding down this volcanic glass to the lustrous sheen of early times. Mirrors of both materials must have been very precious, and it is not surprising that they were used as much for divining purposes as to cater to the vanity of their owners.

The introduction of iron and steel tools has largely destroyed the ancient crafts of wood carving and stone work. Yet two very flourishing crafts survive that may well have had a pre-Columbian origin. A plaster-cloisonné decoration of gourds is carried out at several points along the Central American Highland, and its prototype may be represented in pottery vessels from northwestern Mexico, which are ornamented by similar means. No example of the beautiful lacquer trays from Guerrero and Jalisco survives from the indigenous civilization, but although their pre-Columbian origin may be doubtful, their manufacture was an exclusive Indian property in Colonial times.

ART IN EVERY-DAY LIFE

Thus vestiges of the ancient civilization exist today in some of the modern crafts. Those carvings and buildings which we have grouped under the Fine Arts were really projections of the common technical skill of the people. The virtual anonymity of most religious art fuses the humble crafts with the highest aesthetic expression. The attempts to inculcate "Art in the Home," so often made in modern times, would have been unnecessary in ancient Central America. While the little-known may well present fictitious advantages, particularly in the case of civilizations viewed through the mouse-holes of archaeological research, yet one feels that the Central Americans individually participated in their civilization to a greater extent than we do in ours.

Ornaments of
Pre-Columbian Central America

CENTRAL American ornaments resemble the antique jewelry of Europe in that skilful workmanship contributed more to the value of a piece than the intrinsic worth of the stone or metal. The cost of a jewel was not expressed by its size, as in the case of those modern diamond rings which reflect so clearly the bank notes tendered in payment.

The ancient Central Americans worked, as precious, such stones as jade, turquoise, obsidian, rock crystal, amethyst, opal, beryl, onyx, and carnelian, not to speak of other stones resembling these in textures and color. Around the Isthmus of Panama emeralds were used as ornament, and they have been reported also among the Aztecs. Metals employed for jewelry included gold and copper, but silver ornaments are extremely rare, owing to the metallurgical skill required for extracting the ore. If few of the stones which we moderns consider precious are represented in this list, it should be recalled that the ancient Mediterranean peoples, notably the Egyptians, Greeks, and Romans, knew equally little of our modern gem stones. Their ideas of value were certainly as developed as our own, but to them the sources for modern precious stones were almost completely closed.

The stone most generally esteemed by the Central Americans was jade. The New World varieties are distinguishable from the Asiatic jade, not only in chemical composition, but also in that elusive trait called "feel." Considerable mystery surrounds the exact origin of American jade, because no natural deposits have yet been found in Central America. The few specimens that reveal the original shape of the raw product suggest that jade was collected in boulder form from stream beds but was not mined from the veins. It is quite possible that the more accessible places producing jade have been effectually gleaned of the precious substance by the ancient inhabitants, even as the Spaniards in the Colonial period exhausted the gold deposits which could be worked by hand. From the general distribution of jade objects according to the towns listed in the native manuscripts as paying tribute in that medium, the chief source must have been within the limits of the modern states of Oaxaca, Guerrero, Chiapas, and southern Vera Cruz. Costa Rica also produced much jade ornament, but the workmanship is not comparable to that of the north.

The value of jade to the Central Americans can be authenticated in various ways. The finest work and most skilful sculpture are lavished on objects of this stone. The tribute rolls show a constant demand for jade beads and ornaments. The Nahuan word for jade "chalchihuitl" and its hieroglyph were used with the connotation of "precious," and in describing the adornments of gods and chieftains, the chroniclers refer to jade in the same luscious way that we describe the diamonds of the mighty in our own society. Jade was prominent in the lists of gifts made by the native rulers to the Spaniards at the time of the Conquest. Finally, we have the testimony of the Conquistador, Bernal Diaz, our most engaging first-hand source on the Ancient Mexicans. In describing how the Spaniards looted the treasure of Montezuma's father, previous to their disastrous sortie from Mexico City during the Noche Triste, he says,

" . . . Many of the soldiers of Nar-
vaez and some of our people loaded themselves with it (gold). I declare that I had
no other desire, but the desire to save my
life, but I did not fail to carry off from
some small boxes that were there four
chalchihuites (jades) which are stones very
highly prized among the Indians, and I
quickly placed them in my bosom under
my armor, and later on the price of them
served me well in healing my wounds and
getting me food." No one who has read
*The True History of the Conquest of New
Spain* would ever doubt Bernal Diaz's practical sense of economic values.

Uses of Jade in Central America

The uses of jade were manifold. Axes
and chisels were ground out that were not
only aesthetically pleasing in their polished
symmetry, but also, due to their hardness,
extremely useful in carving softer stones
for major sculptures. Ornaments com-
prised sets of beads, often matched as to
color and size, ear-plugs, and pendants.
Some of the ear-plugs were too large for
human use, and this type of jewelry must
have been made especially for the statues of
the gods. Little pendants often engraved
with floral designs or human figures are
most pleasing, since they combine the
natural luster of the stone with the balance
of design inherent in Central American
craftsmanship.

The process of manufacture must have
been laborious, to judge from the unfin-
ished fragments that have been found.
The jade pebbles were often sawed into
slabs by means of a string of rawhide used
in connection with a rude abrasive like
sand and water. Pecking and grinding
must also have helped to reduce the irregularities of the natural stone. In the Oaxaca
specimens especially, one sees evidence that
a circular drill of bone or reed was used
to engrave many elements of the decorative design. Some of the secondary details
may have been brought out by sharp-

edged flakes of obsidian. Finally the
artisan imparted a lustrous polish to the
specimen.

Main Steps in Working Stone

Prof. M. H. Saville acquired for this
Museum a series of onyx vases that illustrate very neatly the main processes in working stone. First there was the primary
stage of pecking out the block into the
desired external form. The next stage lay
in hollowing the interior by isolating with
a tubular drill thin columns of stone,
which could be readily broken out. A
third step consisted of smoothing off the
irregularities left by pecking and boring.
Then the final details were added, and a
general burnish completed the vessel.
There is no doubt that this general method
applied to the working of all the harder
stones, with the substitution of sawing for
drilling when the need demanded.

Yet the true beauty of jade is expressed
by a series of small sculptures that bring
out in miniature all the consummate design
of the major plastic art. These small
idols, like the Necaxa "tiger" and the
larger votive axe from Vera Cruz, illustrate that element of monumentality which
the better examples of Central American
sculpture possess. By the term "monumentality" I mean the capacity of a carved
figure to be indefinitely enlarged or reduced so that the sculpture, due to the
balance of the elements involved in the
composition, is neither distorted by the
one nor diminished in dignity by the other.
The Necaxa tiger, although only three
inches high, is as impressive as if it were
thirty feet. The Ocosingo jades, representing softer influences from the Maya country, lose nothing in comparison with the
monumental reliefs with which the Mayas
enhanced their stelae and temple walls.
In fact, from our modern point of view,
we can comprehend these minor carvings more readily than the great, since
a *bibelot* one can keep and handle, but mas-

Jade is among the hardest of stones, and was most precious to the ancient Central Americans. They worked it without metal tools, so that the manufacture of ornaments like these must have required months of labor. New World jade can readily be distinguished from the Old World variety

Jade

and

Jadeite

The three jade sculptures shown on this page are among the treasures of the American Museum of Natural History. The middle photograph represents a small figure in the Maya style from Ocosingo, Chiapas. The top and bottom figures represent the same tiger-faced divinity. The seated figure is a little more than three inches high, but the upper one is more than a foot, and is the largest carved jade from Central America. Both carvings may be the work of the semi-mythical Olmecs of Vera Cruz

sive religious sculpture seems to belong to the god in whose honor it was created.

SUBSTITUTES FOR JADE

Many greenish stones, like porphyry, serpentine, and wernerite, the native jewelers worked in a manner similar to jade. Perhaps they could not distinguish these minerals from jade, or perhaps they knew that through the substitution of softer stones they could attain the same effect achieved in the harder and rarer medium. That extraordinary group of sculptures attributable perhaps to the legendary Olmecs depicts people with tiger and baby faces, both in jade and other stones.

The work in rock crystal, due to the excessive hardness of the material, is from the technical point of view even more impressive than the jade sculpture. A few examples exist from various sites of beads and pendants. The most famous example, however, is the nearly life-size skull in the British Museum, and a miniature, illustrated for the first time in these pages, is one of the treasures of the American Museum of Natural History. The rock crystal vase, found by Doctor Caso in Tomb 7 at Monte Alban, represents even more strikingly the days of patient work that the creation of one of these masterpieces must have consumed in the absence of any of our modern mechanical aids.

Ear-plugs and labrets of obsidian (volcanic glass), ground so thin as to be almost transparent, indicate that this useful substance was treated on occasion as a gemstone, and sometimes it was used as a material for sculpture. Even iron pyrites, commonly ground to make mirrors, was at least in one instance carved, as is attested by a lovely example in the Trocadero. Amethyst, opal, carnelian, and the like have been utilized as beads, while turquoise was used above all for mosaic work. The accounts of the loot of the Conquistadores mention emeralds, but they may have been exceptionally fine jades. In fact, of all the stones treated as precious

by the Central Americans, jadeite and nephrite produce the most conspicuous examples of the lapidary's finesse. In civilizations so essentially religious in character as those in Central America, it is to be expected that the work in their most precious stone would produce a sculpture comparable in every way, except size, to the best monumental examples.

Although we have insisted that jade was more valuable than gold to the ancient Central Americans, and Bernal Diaz quotes Montezuma's ambassador as saying "that these rich stones of chalchihuite (jade) . . . were of the highest value, each one being worth more and being esteemed more highly than a great load of gold," this precious metal none the less had value among the Central Americans. Copper was also worked as ornament, but it was more commonly fashioned into tools. On the other hand, gold, save for some sporadic mentions of fishhooks, seems to have been reserved for ornament.

THE ORIGIN OF GOLD WORK TECHNIQUE

The techniques for working gold were apparently invented in northern South America. Indeed, Colombia and Ecuador have produced in sheer bulk the greatest Indian treasures exhumed in the New World. From these countries the gold worker's art spread through Panama to Costa Rica. Perhaps because the sources of the raw metal were negligible, there is no further great development of gold working, until one reaches southern and central Mexico. There we find the cleverest goldsmithing in the New World, although no addition seems to have been made to the fundamental techniques of manufacture imported from the South.

HOW GOLD ORNAMENTS WERE MADE

The Central Americans apparently knew nothing of smelting or other methods of separating the metal from the ore, for they extracted grains and nuggets of gold from river beds. This raw metal they melted

This tiny rock crystal skull represents countless hours of labor, and is one of the three finest specimens in the world. It is probably the work of an Aztec lapidary

Crystal,

Copper, and

Serpentine

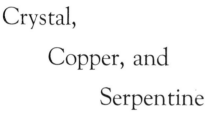

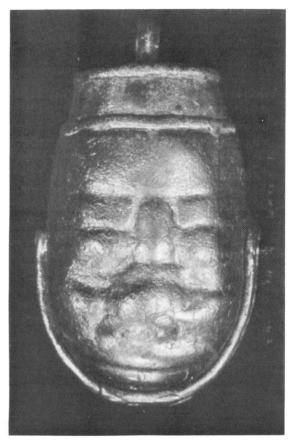

Copper was occasionally used for ornament, as is attested by this large bell sculptured in repoussé. The negroid features suggest a point of origin in southeastern Mexico

The little baby-faced figure to the left resembles the jade figure on page 77. The statuette is of serpentine, and the technique of carving suggests an imitation of the effects obtainable in the harder green stone, jade

This ornament (after Saville, 1920) is an exquisite example of Mixtec jewelry in the National Museum of Mexico. It imitates a feather-mosaic shield and the background of the design is turquoise inlay

Central
American
Goldwork

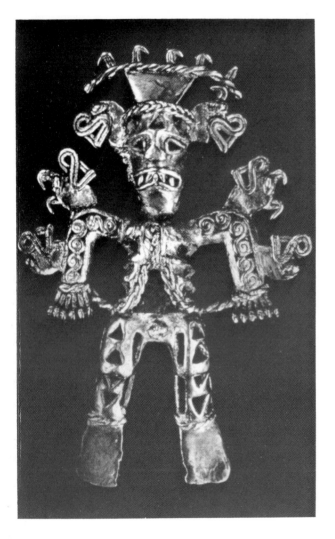

The gold ornaments in the photograph above and at the lower right illustrate the barbaric jewels of Panama and Costa Rica. However, a strong sense of design gives to the four massive brooches a highly decorative effect. The group of five little animals (right, above) is more naturalistic in treatment, although a bird-headed monkey is a beast met more commonly in mythology than in a zoo

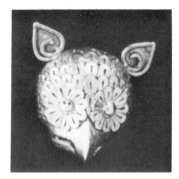

The three little ornaments above (after Saville, 1920) came from Oaxaca, and show the extraordinary skill of the Mixtec goldworkers in their reproduction of a harpy eagle, a monkey, and a horned owl. Note especially the treatment of the owl's feathers. It is a tragedy that so much of this lovely ornament found its way to the Spanish melting pot

down and worked either by hammering or casting. This latter method is extremely ingenious, since it is like the European *cire-perdue* process. The pattern to be cast was engraved on specially treated clay over which was spread a layer of wax. The wax-covered pattern was then coated with more clay through which a wax-filled aperture was made. The mold was then baked, during which process the wax melted and ran out. The molten metal was poured into the resultant cavity, and when the gold had cooled, the mold was broken in order to extract the ornament which, save for a final polishing, was then ready for use.

The Central American goldsmiths knew how to plate copper with gold, and in Mexico they sometimes fused gold and silver into a single ornament. According to contemporary accounts, animals were made with movable legs, and fish with the scales so cunningly jointed that they wriggled. In Mexico they knew how to beat out gold leaf and apply it to objects of wood and stone, while there was considerable work in repoussé, which involves the beating out of a pattern in relief from the reverse of a gold or copper plate.

The regions producing gold ornaments are characterized by various types and styles of presentation. A rich gold art emanates from a chieftain's tomb in the province of Coclé, Panama, scientifically excavated by the archaeologists of the Peabody Museum of Harvard University. Here delightful animal figures contrast with the austerity of heavy ornaments and ceremonial discs in repoussé. Another group of gold objects comes from Costa Rica in the magnificent collection of Minor C. Keith, half of which is on view in the American Museum of Natural History. There are close parallels between this art and that of Panama, and here also one may enjoy the fresh vitality of little animals like frogs, crabs, and armadillos, as well as marvel at the bulk of formal ornament. An earring representing an animal

seated in a swing indicates a quaint humanitarianism unwilling to allow even an ornamental beast to dangle by its neck. A whole collection of birds of various sizes could serve as models to jewelers today, so marked is the *chic* of the cleverly conventionalized forms. There is a considerable amount of copper plating and copper alloy that attest to some skill in metallurgy.

In the region occupied by the great Maya cities, there has appeared even less gold than jade, and both seem to owe their presence to trade. The Sacred Well at Chichen Itza, source of the greatest treasure hitherto found in the Maya area, yielded gold ornaments obtained from as far as Costa Rica to the southeast and southern Mexico to the southwest. It is not until the frontier between the Highland and Maya cultures is reached that we find the great development of gold working.

NOTABLE EXAMPLES OF GOLD WORK

According to Prof. M. H. Saville, whose *Goldsmith's Art in Ancient Mexico* is the authoritative work on this subject, northern Oaxaca produced more notable gold objects than any other section of Mexico, and this statement was made before the discovery of the treasure in Tomb 7 at Monte Alban. Nor can this rich harvest be entirely due to the drain put by the Spaniards on other parts of Mexico, since they were as active in Oaxaca as anywhere else. A soldier named Figueroa, according to Bernal Diaz, gave up trying to conquer the Indian tribes of Mixteca and "determined to undertake the excavation of graves in the burial places of the Caciques of these provinces, for he found in them a quantity of gold jewels . . . and he attained such dexterity that he took out from these over five thousand pesos de oro in addition to other jewels obtained from the pueblos." The enormous yield of Doctor Caso's remarkable discovery at Monte Alban gives an idea of the scope of the gold-worker's industry there. Finger rings, to wear below the knuckle and at the first joint, bore representations of eagles executed in filigree. Necklaces arranged in decorative tiers and massive gorgets depicting gods and religious symbols gave evidence of a sumptuous ceremonialism. Pearls also were scattered about the tomb and innumerable fragments of turquoise attested to disintegrated mosaics. Sophisticated as was the subject matter of the Monte Alban jewels, the outlines of some of the gorgets show the southern ancestry of the goldsmith's art in Oaxaca.

MUSEUM PIECES

The collections of the American Museum reveal a few consummate examples of gold work. A small owl's head, complete even to the overlapping feathers, corroborates the tales of the Conquistadores and shows a technical precision not unworthy to be compared with Benvenuto Cellini's artistry. A haughty little harpy eagle head combines naturalism with a strong sense of decorative values, and a large lip ornament representing an eagle head subordinates naturalistic detail to design, without distorting the essential realism of the reproduction. Even beads are carefully worked into forms which are as satisfactory individually as they are when grouped as a necklace.

The Aztec gold work, thanks to the assiduous looting of the Spaniards, has almost completely disappeared. We know that there was a guild of goldsmiths, high in social standing, who inhabited a special quarter of Azcapotzalco and claimed descent from the legendary Toltecs. Conspicuous

in the tribute sent by Cortes to his king was a golden "wheel" six and a half feet in diameter, inscribed like the famous "calendar stone" with the sun, day signs, and other symbolic elements relating to time as recorded by the Aztecs. Cortes was also the recipient of a necklace in which golden scorpions were a conspicuous element. How far the Aztec goldsmiths were influenced by Oaxacan styles the dearth of specimens from the Valley of Mexico prevents our saying, but in the lists of Spanish loot there is a general correspondence between the descriptions of the Aztec treasure and the different types of ornament recovered in Oaxaca.

The jeweler's art in Central America, as can be seen by the illustrations accompanying this article, is capably developed and appears less alien to our modern tastes than the major arts. Personal eclecticism and the joy of individual possession influence one's taste in ornament to a great degree. A contributory factor in the appreciation of an art is the possibility of incorporating examples in one's own milieu, a condition difficult to envisage with the major examples of Central American arts. However, to keep as a *bibelot* a jade ornament, or to wear a gold idol as a brooch or charm is perfectly feasible, since such an action involves no violent adjustment of aesthetic or ideological conceptions. Perhaps the sheer craftsmanship of the Central American jewel worker will lead us to as close an appreciation of Central American art as any other factor in these remarkable civilizations.

The Pottery of
Pre-Columbian Central America

THE potter's art in Central America reveals an extraordinary development of imaginative skill. It seems little bound by those set requirements of ritual which governed artistic expression in the arts we have considered in the five preceding chapters. Humble as are the uses of pottery, an almost infinite invention is displayed by the multiplicity of forms and decorative styles. The work in clay suggests that here the oppressive grasp of religion was relinquished, releasing the fancy thwarted in other directions. No other part of the world, China not excepted, shows such diverse forms and decorations as those displayed by pre-Columbian ceramics in the area between Chile and the Rio Grande.

In Central America, as elsewhere, the invention and practice of agriculture relieved man from his unremitting search for food, since the harvest created a store to satisfy his needs for months to come. The leisure thus gained gave him a chance to use his mind in directions other than the hunt, and led to the series of inventions and intellectual conceptions which culminated in the handful of great World Civilizations. One of the first steps taken by the early farmer was to devise means of conserving his winter food supply and of preparing it for palatable consumption. In the attainment of these ends, the development of containers of baked clay played a significant and highly important part.

Apart from its importance as an invention, pottery has a more complete historical record than any other phase of early culture in Central America. The hardness of baked clay renders it relatively immune from the destructive action of rot or fire, which have so affected textiles and wooden objects.

Even when a vessel is broken, the fragments survive among the ruins of a building or in the village refuse heap. The lack of intrinsic value secured pottery from the cupidity of invaders, greedy for treasure. The common household functions of ceramic products cleared them of the stigma of heretical barbarism, which impelled the Conquistadores to destroy so much of the native religious art in Central America. The usefulness of pottery made it a usual equipment for the dead in their life beyond the grave, so that many complete examples have been conserved in burials, to satisfy later the rapacious curiosity of excavators. Thus the study of pottery, because it is both prevalent and indestructible, has become the backbone of archaeological technique, and by means of the local and tribal decorative styles it is possible to trace the history of early peoples by the fragments of their vessels. Unfortunately, the involved descriptions of pots and pans, which in consequence fill professional reports on excavations, effectively quench whatever interest the layman might take in them.

To absorb the full beauty of Central American ceramic form and design, one must look beyond the borders of the Greek aesthetic ideal. The exquisite shapes of Greek vases resulted from the harmonious principles devised to govern the proportions of their vessels, but lovely as were the results, these formulae restricted the range of forms. Central American pottery, in contrast, seems completely without such laws, so varied are the shapes. A more detailed examination discloses, however, the operation of rigorous local customs to which the potters strictly adhered. As the pueblo, or town, was the chief unit of group organization, there arose almost innumerable local

This vase from Miahuatlan, Oaxaca, represents
Macuilxochitl, the Mexican god of games and
feasting. The simple lines of the vessel throw
into vivid prominence the lively figure of the
divinity. The design on his loin cloth and his
necklace of gold and jade are faithfully represented

Ceremonial Vessel
from Mexico

Left: This vase from Tepic, Mexico, (after Lumholtz, 1902) represents a turkey. The wing feathers and wattles of the neck are picked out in gold leaf

Below: Guatemala was the source of this elaborately carved vase (after Saville, 1919) which is a masterpiece of Maya ceramics

Below: The glazed effect of this type of Salvador pottery was so greatly admired in ancient Central America that it was traded far and wide. This delightful example shows how successfully the potter animated the vessel by the use of a few simple lines

Above: This sturdy jar from western Mexico illustrates the architectural proportions of much Central American pottery. Structure is stressed, rather than concealed, as Central American art is relatively little concerned with ephemeral grace

Below: The pottery of Costa Rica is often lavishly ornamented, but in these examples painted designs are used to emphasize simple effigy forms. Note how the jars are supported in one case by a tripod, in the other by an annular base

Above: This vase from one of the earliest Central American cultures shows how excellent decorative effects could be attained by the use of a lustrous surface and a few simple lines

styles, differing widely from one another and giving to the whole of Central America the effect of aesthetic anarchy, so far as pottery is concerned.

While the shapes of Greek vases give the effect of defeating gravity by their graceful upward curves, the Central American potters seem to stress the difficulty of keeping their vessels erect. The greatest dimension is apt to be horizontal, rather than vertical, and emphasis is placed on the support which in the smaller vessels is usually a ring base or three or (less commonly) four legs. So constant is the use of a low center of gravity that vases with the "soaring" quality of the Greek urn are almost unknown. It is possible that the technical difficulties of building up a vessel with strips of wet clay may have necessitated a more solid structure than that demanded by the more rapid Greek process of throwing up a vessel on the potter's wheel.

The shapes of Central American pottery are as eminently satisfying as the forms of natural objects. Some bowls are almost spherical and others have the form of a pear. Cylindrical vases of varying dimensions express a delicate grace if tall and narrow, or practical solidity if short and wide. By curving the walls slightly inward or outward, beautiful variations are obtained. Again, a bowl may be grooved to give the effect of a gourd, or else ridged spirally to bring up the high lights on its surface. Many vessels are made in two sections, a wall and base, and, by increasing the size of one or the other, not only are various delightful proportions attained, but also fields are created for a rich variety of decorative effects. In western Mexico occur especially attractive forms, which involve a curved base, with an almost horizontal shoulder, out of which protrudes a flaring neck.

The simplest form of decoration is to polish the exterior of the vessel. The methods of firing the pots seldom produce an absolutely even color, so that the glossy surfaces suggest the tones of polished fruits or the glossy coats of animals. Black, for example, is seldom jet black, but more the shade of well-used walnut furniture. Reds range from the brown tones of a russet apple to the solid shades of red peppers, dried and polished. Browns merge into black at one extreme and dwindle through imperceptible gradations to a matt yellow. Warm orange tones characterize the clays of several ceramic families, while others show steely gray shades. Such lustrous tones enhance the pure forms in a way that painting never can.

There are numerous cases of effigy vessels, where in the simplest stages, a head, limbs, and tail, added to the pot, give it a pleasingly alive appearance. Sometimes the head alone is added and the anatomical details are incised. In extreme cases the animation of a pot is carried so far that it becomes a sculpture in clay, like the figures of western Mexico mentioned in a previous chapter. The most consistent use of effigy pottery is in the Plumbate Ware of Salvador, which has a vitreous surface and is the nearest approach to true glaze in Central America.

Since the tripod support was so important in keeping a vessel on an even keel, the Central American potter gave vent to his imagination in constructing this useful adjunct. One way was to make the legs hollow and insert pellets of clay, so that they became rattles. Often the supports were modeled into imitations of animal or human legs, and sometimes, in Costa Rica, Atlantean figures supported the bowl. The modeling of bird and animal heads was also thought a suitable means of transforming a functional necessity into an ornament. When a ring base was used, it was often painted or carved, and sometimes by closing the bottom, it was converted into a rattle.

Two other methods of decoration were in general use. One was to produce a decorative effect on the surface of the pot by incision or applying bits of clay. The second was to add a painted design. Which of the two was the earlier there is no means of knowing, since no really primitive culture has yet been discovered in Central America. If the cultures of the Southwestern United States, which

Mexican Design

The sources for Mexican pottery designs are many and varied. In the upper right hand picture the purely conventional *grecque* is used, whereas the vase at the lower right is ornamented by the hieroglyph for one of the days of their month, which is a conventional representation of the reed. The jar at the upper left is ornamented in plaster cloisonné, and the central band (after Lumholtz, 1902) reproduces the design from a similar vessel. Such stylized human figures are rare in Mexican ornament

Above: This cover from a Zapotec incense burner shows the transformation of a vessel into a ceremonial sculpture

Left: The incensario at the left is much restored and comes from the Teotihuacan culture of the Valley of Mexico. It shows the building-up process utilized in this class of religious vessel

Below: This clay mask from Vera Cruz is a simple and straightforward piece of sculpture, yet it may have been used in connection with some elaborate creation like that on the left

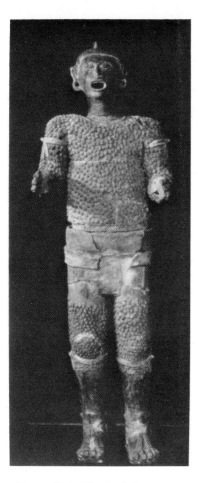

Above: This life-sized figure from the Valley of Mexico is a remarkable technical achievement, requiring great skill in building up the sections so that they would not collapse of their own weight

The head at the upper right was one of a pair of effigy vases found with a burial of the Mazapan culture at Teotihuacan. Although treated sculpturally it is none the less a container. The large figure at its left, and the seated figure from Nayarit are pure sculptures. The photographs on these pages show in striking fashion the contrast between convention and naturalism in Central American art

showed the transition between hunters and agriculturists, produced painted designs as the earliest ceramic decoration, the Argentine and the Eastern United States were the home of primitive tribes who incised and stamped their rude vessels. Therefore, in describing Central American ceramic decoration, we cannot follow an evolutionary plan.

Incising and carving the surface of a bowl were especially common. The cruder examples, from the earliest cultures yet found, show simple geometric patterns made sometimes after sun drying and occasionally after the pot was baked. A striking development of this process was the Teotihuacan method of champlevé, in which, after a vessel had been fired and burnished, the polished surface was cut away to leave a figure in relief. Sometimes the effect was enhanced by rubbing red pigment into this roughened background. Some of the finest reliefs in the Maya country may be found on carved vases of this type from Yucatan, where great skill in sculpture and drawing raised the champlevé work from the secondary field of decoration to the primary one of Fine Art.

A type of decoration which is found in western Mexico and perhaps derived from this work in champlevé approaches the technique of cloisonné. In the Mexican examples a completed pot was covered with plaster and the desired design outlined by scraping the soft exterior down to the original surface of the pot. Into these scraped zones, plaster strips of different colors were laid, creating a harmonious, if fragile, decoration. Another method of ornament involved a covering of plaster, which was then painted in fresco. These plaster decorations could not have survived daily use and must have required special treatment for mortuary or ceremonial use. In fact, in several examples, a painted design has been concealed by a covering of fresco or plaster cloisonné.

Another decorative style consisted of pressing a stamped design on to the wet surface of a bowl. This process, when repeated, gave a symmetrical series of orna-

ments in relief or intaglio. Even commoner was the attachment of decorative elements made in moulds, which might represent floral patterns, human and animal heads, or else purely conventional designs. Clay vessels were sometimes touched up with gold leaf, like the celebrated Tepic effigy vase, and clay beads treated in the same way were thrifty imitations of the real thing.

Painted decoration involved a prevalent use of geometric design. As we have suggested in the section on Crafts, there is very strong evidence that the textile art with its complementary ornamental patterns was developed long before pottery. Since, in the Southwestern United States the designs painted on pottery are in direct imitation of the earlier basketry patterns, there is considerable likelihood that this practice was quite general in the New World. There was no orderly evolution of design from naturalism into conventionalization. The use of naturalistic elements appeared late, strictly governed by the requirements of harmonious design.

The arrangement of the design in most localities was in panels. Frequently these design units, when on the outside of the bowl, were arranged in threes, so that a complete pattern could be seen. This principle is based on a "rule of thumb" geometry, since a little less than a third of a cylindrical body can be viewed from the side. Continuous patterns, except for borders, are much less common. Besides the steps, grecques and volutes of geometric design, there were also conventionalizations of natural forms. Flowers, animals, hieroglyphs, religious symbols, were cunningly treated to make decorative effects. In the Maya pottery of Copan and Salvador the monkey was often used, since its elongated arms and tail were readily adaptable to the needs of design.

The colors include shades of white, red, yellow, orange, black, with occasional uses of blue and green. The disposition of the colors usually involves one for the background, another to outline the design, and a third to fill the patterns. Sometimes when

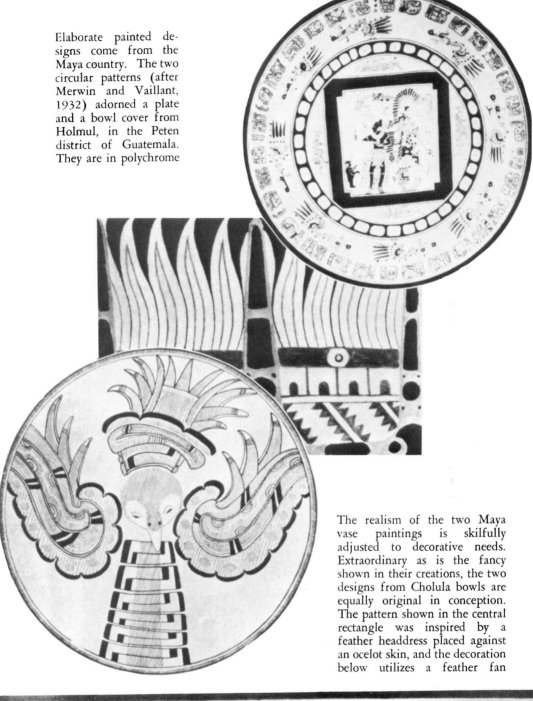

Elaborate painted designs come from the Maya country. The two circular patterns (after Merwin and Vaillant, 1932) adorned a plate and a bowl cover from Holmul, in the Peten district of Guatemala. They are in polychrome

The realism of the two Maya vase paintings is skilfully adjusted to decorative needs. Extraordinary as is the fancy shown in their creations, the two designs from Cholula bowls are equally original in conception. The pattern shown in the central rectangle was inspired by a feather headdress placed against an ocelot skin, and the decoration below utilizes a feather fan

Maya
Pottery
Designs

Left: The Maya used their script in decorative fashion. This vase from Guatemala, like the Holmul plate on the preceding page, utilizes bands of glyphs to divide off design fields

Below: The conventionalized pelican on this vase is carried out in red tones on a white background. This and the upper vase are after Gordon, 1925-28

Left: This vase from Salvador is ornamented by designs in black and orange on a yellow field, while the Maya bowls on the preceding page show similar uses of warm red and orange tones with black outlines

realistic elements like a headdress or a butterfly are portrayed, they are used naturalistically. The fullest use of naturalism in color and design is in the celebrated "picture" vases from the Maya country which we have considered under Painting.

Besides pottery vessels, the work in baked clay extends to many other types of objects. The figurine cult, which contributes so much to the plastic art of Central America, absorbed much of the potter's inventiveness. Spindle whorls, the weights used for the wooden shafts in spinning cotton, become, in the hands of Central Mexican clay workers, beautiful little creations, with their lustrous red or black slips and delicately worked reliefs. The stamps for adorning cloth or the skin are often of clay, and represent in their cutting skilful judgment of balanced design. Musical instruments like whistles, flutes and ocarinas require of the potter a knowledge of the physical properties of tone, while the cylindrical drums of Central America are often beautifully ornamented by carving or painting. A curious musical instrument, very rarely found, is the whistling jar which gives out a note by the air expelled when the liquid is poured out. The massive incensarios, used to burn incense before the temples, are as imposing from a structural point of view as from one of ceremonial art. Pipes, used presumably for ceremonial smoking, since cigarettes and cigars were the usual method for consuming tobacco, are frequently exquisitely polished and very well proportioned. Censers or incense ladles often received treatment comparable to the best of the ceremonial art.

The relationship of these Central American clay forms to the art of the present day brings one face to face with the besetting difficulty of modern European art. We are in an age of revolution, intellectual and artistic as well as political and technical. There is a tendency to abandon individualism for group action, and, in the fields of architecture and the decorative arts, function and the relationship between the material and the form tend to suppress the individualism of the craftsman's personal expression. The copying of alien art forms is arid when it is not jarring, so that it would be stupid to utilize in our art today the *content* of Central American aesthetic expression. On the other hand, the impersonality of Central American art, which expresses a mass life under divine direction, dovetails well with our modern disciplines under mass production and mass movement.

Our recent World Fairs, intended for the absorption of millions of people, produces the anonymous effect of the work of thousands of artisans and engineers, but not the genius of an individual. Much this same spirit permeates the art of Central America. The principles of design and form are no less inherent in our discipline by graph, blue print, and mathematical formula than in the ancient Central American rule by ritual.

This and the preceding chapters have been intended to show the various aspects of Central American art without insistence on the complicated historical background. The relationship of the individual Central American to his art we can probably never know precisely, although we can be certain it was not aesthetic in our modern sense of the word. On the other hand, we moderns can extract a great deal of pleasure, even inspiration, from the contemplation of the works of these gifted people, if we lay aside the tenets and traditions of our past art history to examine Central American art from the viewpoint of our modern industrial age.

BIBLIOGRAPHY

The following list of books on Central American archaeology comprises volumes in English of general interest to the layman which are likely to be accessible in public libraries or else purchasable at moderate cost. Many of these volumes contain extensive bibliographies, so that the more deeply interested reader may find his way to the more technical publications in English and foreign languages. By far the best introduction to Central American archaeology is Doctor H. J. Spinden's *Ancient Civilizations of Mexico and Central America*, published in the Handbook Series of this Museum. Many articles of popular interest on Central America are to be found in *Natural History*.

BANCROFT, H. H.
1883.   The Native Races. 5 vols. San Francisco, 1883.

BLOM, F. AND LA FARGE, O.
1926.   Tribes and Temples. A Record of the Expedition to Middle America Conducted by the Tulane University of Louisiana in 1925 (The Tulane University of Louisiana, 2 vols., New Orleans, 1926).

CAHILL, HOLGER
1933.   American Sources of Modern Art (The Museum of Modern Art, May 11 to June 30, 1933. Catalogue of Exhibition, New York, 1933).

CHARNAY, DÉSIRÉ
1888.   The Ancient Cities of the New World, being Voyages and Explorations in Mexico and Central America from 1857-1882. New York, 1888.

CORTES, HERNANDO
1908.   Letters of Cortes (Translated and edited by F. A. MacNutt). 2 vols. New York, 1908.

DAVIS, EMILY C.
1931.   Ancient Americans. The Archaeological Story of Two Continents. New York, 1931.

DIAZ DEL CASTILLO, B.
1908-1916.   The True History of the Conquest of New Spain, 5 vols. Edited and published in Mexico by Genaro Garcia. Translated by A. P. Maudslay (Hakluyt Society, Series II, vols. 23-25, 30, 40, London, 1908-1916).

GANN, T. W. AND THOMPSON, J. E.
1931.   History of the Maya; from the Earliest Times to the Present Day. New York, 1931.

HOLMES, W. H.
1895 and 1897. Archaeological Studies Among the Ancient Cities of Mexico (Field Columbian Museum, Anthropological Series No. 8, vol. 1, parts 1 and 2, Chicago, 1895 and 1897).

JOYCE, T. A.
1920.   Mexican Archaeology. An introduction to the Archaeology of the Mexican and Mayan Civilizations of Pre-Spanish America. London, 1920.

JOYCE, T. A.
1927.   Maya and Mexican Art. London, 1927.
LINNÉ, S.
1934.   Archaeological Researches at Teotihuacan, Mexico (The
                   Ethnographical Museum of Sweden, new series, Publica-
                   tion No. 1, Stockholm, 1934).
LOTHROP, S. K.
1926.   Pottery of Costa Rica and Nicaragua (Contributions, Mu-
                   seum of the American Indian, Heye Foundation, vol.
                   8, 2 vols., New York, 1926).
LUMHOLTZ, C.
1902.   Unknown Mexico. 2 vols. New York, 1902.
MORLEY, S. G.
1915.   An Introduction to the Study of Maya Hieroglyphs (Bulletin
                   57, Bureau of American Ethnology, Washington, 1915).
1920.   The Inscriptions at Copan (Carnegie Institution of Washing-
                   ton, Publication 219, Washington, 1920).
MORRIS, ANN AXTELL
1931.   Digging in Yucatan. New York, 1931.
PRESCOTT, W. H.
1922.   The Conquest of Mexico. Edited by T. A. Joyce and illus-
                   trated by Keith Henderson. 2 vols. New York, 1922.
RADIN, P.
1920.   The Sources and Authenticity of the History of the Ancient
                   Mexicans (University of California Publications in
                   American Archaeology and Ethnology, vol. 17, no. 1,
                   pp. 1-150, Berkeley, 1920).
REDFIELD, R.
1930.   Tepoztlan: a Mexican Village. A Study of Folk Life (The
                   University of Chicago Publications in Anthropology,
                   Ethnological Series, Chicago, 1930).
SPENCE, L.
1923.   The Gods of Mexico. London, 1923.
SPINDEN, H. J.
1913.   A Study of Maya Art, its Subject Matter and Historical
                   Development (Memoirs, Peabody Museum of American
                   Archaeology and Ethnology, Harvard University, vol.
                   6, Cambridge, 1913).
1928.   Ancient Civilizations of Mexico and Central America (Hand-
                   book Series, no. 3, American Museum of Natural History.
                   Third and revised edition. New York, 1928).
STEPHENS, J. L.
1841.   Incidents of Travel in Central America, Chiapas, and Yuca-
                   tan. 2 vols. New York, 1841.
1843.   Incidents of Travel in Yucatan. 2 vols. New York, 1843.
TEEPLE, J. E.
1930.   Maya Astronomy (Contributions to American Archaeology,
                   No. 2, Carnegie Institution of Washington, Publication
                   403, pp. 29-115, Washington, 1930).

THOMPSON, J. ERIC
    1933.   Mexico Before Cortez. An Account of the Daily Life, Religion, and Ritual of the Aztecs and Kindred Peoples. New York, 1933.

TOTTEN, GEORGE OAKLEY
    1926.   Maya Architecture. Washington, 1926.

VAILLANT, GEORGE C.
    1939.   Indian Arts in North America. New York, 1939.

WILLARD, T. A.
    1926.   The City of the Sacred Well. Being a Narrative of the Discoveries and Excavations of Edward Herbert Thompson in the Ancient City of Chi-Chen Itza with some Discourse on the Culture and Development of the Mayan Civilization as Revealed by Their Art and Architecture. New York, 1926.

WISSLER, CLARK
    1938.   The American Indian. An introduction to the Anthropology of the New World. Third Edition. New York, 1938.

SOURCES OF ILLUSTRATIONS REPRODUCED IN THE TEXT

Caso, A.

1927.   Las Ruinas de Tizatlan, Tlaxcala (Revista Mexicana de Estudios Historicos, vol. 1, pp. 139-172, Mexico, 1927).

Catherwood, F.

1844.   Views of Ancient Monuments in Central America, Chiapas and Yucatan. London, 1844.

Charnay, Désiré

1862-1863.   Cités et Ruines Américaines. Mitla, Palenqué, Izamal, Chichen-Itza, Uxmal. Recueilles et Photographiées par Désiré Charnay. Avec un Texte par (Eugène Emmanuel) Viollet-Le-Duc, Ferdinand Denis. Suivi du Voyage et des Documents de l'Auteur. Paris, 1862-1863.

Codices

Codex Borbonicus

1899.   Manuscrit Mexicain de la Bibliothèque du Palais-Bourbon, publié en fac-simile, avec un commentaire explicatif par E. T. Hamy. Paris, 1899.

Codex Boturini

Reproduced in Radin, P., Sources and Authenticity of the History of Ancient Mexico (University of California Publications in American Archaeology and Ethnology, vol. 17, no. 1, pp. 1-150, Berkeley, 1920).

Codex Nuttall or Codex Zouche

1902.   Facsimile of an Ancient Mexican Codex belonging to Lord Zouche of Harynworth, with an introduction by Zelia Nuttall (Peabody Museum of Archaeology and Ethnology, Harvard University, Cambridge, 1902).

Codex Telleriano-Remensis

1899.   Codex Telleriano Remensis, Manuscrit Mexicain. Reproduit en photochromographie aux frais du Duc de Loubat et précédé d'une Introduction contenant la Transcription complète des Anciens Commentaires Hispano-Mexicans. . . . par E. T. Hamy. Paris, 1899.

Codex Vindobonensis (Vienna Codex) Codex Vindobonensis Mexic. 1. Facsimileausgabe der Mexikanischen Bilder-Handschrift der Nationalbibliothek in Wien (Lehmann, Walter und Smital, Ottokar). Wien, 1929.

Lienzo de Tlaxcala

Reproduced in Antigüedades Mexicanas publicadas por la Junta Colombina de Mexico en el cuarto centenario de descubrimento de América. Mexico, 1892.

Tribute Roll of Montezuma

Reproduced in Peñafiel, A. Monumentos del Arte Mexicano Antiguo. 3 vols. Berlin, 1890.

DIESELDORFF, E. P.
    1904.   A Pottery Vase with Figure Painting, from a Grave in Chama (Bulletin 28, Bureau of American Ethnology, pp. 635-644, Washington, 1904).

DUPAIX, G.
    1834.   Antiquités Mexicaines. Relation des Trois Expéditions du Capitaine Dupaix ordonnées en 1805, 1806, et 1807, pour la Recherche des Antiquités du Pays, notamment celles de Mitla et de Palenque. 2 vols. and atlas. Paris, 1834.

GAMIO, M.
    1922.   La Poblacion del Valle de Teotihuacan (Secretaria de Agricultura y Fomento, Direccion de Antropologia, tomo 1, vols. 1 and 2, tomo 2, Mexico, 1922).

GORDON, G. B. (editor)
    1925-1928   Examples of Maya Pottery in the Museum and other Collections (The University Museum, University of Pennsylvania, Philadelphia, 1925-1928).

HEGER, FRANZ
    1908.   Der Altamerikanische Federschmuck in den Sammlungen der anthropologisch-ethnographischen Abteilung des k. k. naturhistorischen Hofmuseums in Wien (Festschrift herausgegeben anläszlich d. Tagung d. XVI Internationalen Amerikanisten-Kongresses in Wien, September 1908, vom Organisations-komitee. Wien, 1908).

HOLMES, W. H.
    1895 and 1897. Archaeological Studies among the Ancient Cities of Mexico (Field Columbian Museum, Publication No. 8, Anthropological Series, vol. 1, no. 1, parts 1 and 2, Chicago, 1895 and 1897).
    1914-1915.   Masterpieces of Aboriginal American Art (Art and Archaeology, vol. 1, pp. 1-12, 91-102, 243-255, Washington, 1914-1915).

HUMBOLDT, A.
    1810.   Vues des Cordillères et Monuments des Peuples Indigènes de l'Amérique. Paris, 1810.

JOYCE, T. A.
    1927.   Maya and Mexican Art. London, 1927.

LEHMANN, W.
    1933.   Aus den Pyramidenstädten in Alt-Mexiko. Berlin, 1933.

LOTHROP, S. K.
    1924.   Tulum. An Archaeological Study of the East Coast of Yucatan (Carnegie Institution of Washington, Publication 335, Washington, 1924).

LUMHOLTZ, C.
    1902.   Unknown Mexico. 2 vols. New York, 1902.

MALER, T.
1908.   Explorations in the Department of Peten, Guatemala, and
                 Adjacent Region (Memoirs, Peabody Museum of Ameri-
                 can Archaeology and Ethnology, vol. 4, no. 1, Cambridge,
                 1908).
1911.   Explorations in the Department of Peten, Guatemala. Tikal
                 (Memoirs, Peabody Museum of American Archaeology and
                 Ethnology, Harvard University, vol. 5, no. 1, Cambridge,
                 1911).
MASON, J. A. (editor)
1928.   Examples of Maya Pottery in the Museum and other Collec-
                 tions (The University Museum, University of Pennsyl-
                 vania, Philadelphia, 1928).
MAUDSLAY, A. P.
1889-1902.   Biologia Centrali-Americana, or Contributions to the Knowl-
                 edge of the Flora and Fauna of Mexico and Central
                 America. Archaeology, 4 vols. of text and plates. London,
                 1889-1902.
MERWIN, B. E. AND VAILLANT, G. C.
1932.   The Ruins of Holmul, Guatemala (Memoirs, Peabody Mu-
                 seum of Harvard University, vol. 3, no. 2, Cambridge,
                 1932).
MORRIS, E. H., WITH CHARLOT, J., AND MORRIS, A. A.
1931.   The Temple of the Warriors at Chichen Itza, Yucatan (Car-
                 negie Institution of Washington, Publication 406, 2 vols.
                 Washington, 1931).
PRESCOTT, W. H.
1922.   The Conquest of Mexico. Edited by T. A. Joyce and illus-
                 trated by Keith Henderson. 2 vols. New York, 1922.
SAVILLE, M. H.
1919.   A Sculptured Vase from Guatemala (Leaflets, no. 1, Museum
                 of the American Indian, Heye Foundation, New York,
                 1919).
1920.   The Goldsmith's Art in Ancient Mexico (Indian Notes and
                 Monographs, Museum of the American Indian, Heye
                 Foundation, New York, 1920).
1922.   Turquoise Mosaic Art in Ancient Mexico (Contributions,
                 Museum of the American Indian, Heye Foundation,
                 vol. 6, New York, 1922).
1925.   The Wood-Carver's Art in Ancient Mexico (Contributions,
                 Museum of the American Indian, Heye Foundation,
                 vol. 9, New York, 1925).
SMITH, A. LEDYARD
1932.   Two Recent Ceramic Finds at Uaxactun (Contributions to
                 American Archaeology, no. 5, Carnegie Institution of
                 Washington, Publication 436, pp. 1-25, Washington, 1932).
TOTTEN, GEORGE OAKLEY
1926.   Maya Architecture. Washington, 1926.